A LIFE WORTH LIVING

AND A LORD WORTH LOVING

A Life Worth Living

and A Lord Worth Loving

Stuart
Olyott

 EVANGELICAL PRESS

EVANGELICAL PRESS
12 Wooler Street, Darlington, Co. Durham, DL1 1RQ, England

First published 1983
Second impression 1986
Third impression 1992

ISBN 0 85234 124 5

Other books by Stuart Olyott:

The Three are One
The Gospel as it Really is (WCS)
Dare to Stand Alone (WCS)
You Might Have Asked ... about the Christian Faith
Son of Mary, Son of God

Printed and bound in Great Britain by the Bath Press, Bath, Avon

To the elders, deacons and members of
Belvidere Road Church, Liverpool,
with affectionate thanks for fifteen years
of fellowship and mutual support in the
things of God.

Contents

Introduction

For years I had a Bible with two books missing. They had been printed all right, but I never read them. I could not make head nor tail of them, and so ignored them. For all practical purposes they did not exist. Not unnaturally, my spiritual life was stunted, for my Lord had declared, 'Man shall not live by bread alone, but by *every* word that proceedeth out of the mouth of God' (Matthew 4:4).

Three books helped to put things right for me. They did not explain everything, but got me to *read* the neglected books for myself. Chief among them was Irving L. Jensen's *Self-Study Guide* on the two books, published by Moody Press. Then there was *The Wycliffe Bible Commentary*, also published by Moody Press, with its brief commentaries by Robert Laurin and Sierd Woudstra. Finally there was the 1954 edition of *The New Bible Commentary* published by the Inter-Varsity Fellowship, with its similarly brief but helpful commentary on the Song of Solomon by Professor W.J. Cameron.

I am no longer scared of Ecclesiastes and the Song of Solomon, and my Bible is complete! Remembering what brief commentaries have done in my own experience, it seemed sensible to produce another which was not hidden away in larger volumes. As you would expect, it owes a lot to the titles above, with the publishers' permission. But what does that matter? If it gets you to read two almost forgotten books, and restores them to *your* Bible, its production will have been more than worthwhile.

May none of us rest content until 'every word' of God's Word is written in our memories, loved in our hearts and practised in our lives!

STUART OLYOTT,
Lausanne,

A life worth living:
Ecclesiastes

1.
Some things to say first

Importance

The poetical book we are about to read was written almost 3,000 years ago. That in itself should fill us with interest. But we cannot study it like other books from the ancient world. It is part of the sacred Scriptures, of which the inspired apostle declared, 'Whatsoever things were written aforetime were written for our learning, that we through patience and comfort of the scriptures might have hope' (Romans 15:4).

Ecclesiastes was written for *us*, and we cannot ignore it without impoverishing ourselves. Its style is not quite what we are used to, but its message is plain. It tells us what kind of living is worthwhile. This it does by a process of reasonings, reflections, observations and conclusions, all encapsuled in pithy and brief lines of poetry. There is a wonderful freshness about it all. What it says is so startlingly relevant that we find it hard to believe that it was not written *today*.

Key

In this book Solomon looks at life from two viewpoints. First of all he stands in one position, and then in the other, and does this alternately throughout the book. He sees the same issues from two perspectives. It is virtually impossible to make any sense of Ecclesiastes unless this simple fact has been grasped first.

Solomon's first viewpoint is that of a natural man. He

13

sees life through the eyes of a person who is still unconverted. Such a person tackles life's problems without the light of God's revelation. He leaves God out of the picture, and never ponders his Word. The only conclusion he can come to is that 'All is vanity' (1:2). Everything in this mortal life is ultimately futile. It is a waste of time.

Solomon's other viewpoint is radically different. He now looks at life through the eyes of a man to whom God has revealed himself. Such a person sees everything in a new light. Life has meaning after all, but only if we worship and serve God. When he stands in this position, Solomon's words ring with assurance and hope. The dark beginning of the book sees Solomon occupying the first perspective; the bright conclusion sees him enjoying the other.

But *how* can we know God? Ecclesiastes stirs up this question in our minds, but does not give us the answer. It leaves us hungry to know God, but does not show us the way to him. That is something which is revealed only in the gospel of our Lord Jesus Christ, and part of the purpose of Ecclesiastes is to prepare us to receive it. It shows to us that man's search for truth gets him nowhere. The path of the philosophers is a no through road. The meaning of life is not found by observing and recording our experiences. Nor is it discovered by following through our thoughts. God, who alone gives human life its purpose, cannot be known unless he reveals himself. The book makes us long for him to do so, and all who understand its message greet the gospel with relief and excitement.

Structure

The book opens with a short introduction (1:1-11). Its main point is to state that, from the human point of view, 'all is vanity'. This note will be struck again and again, throughout the book, even when we are on the very threshold of its ultimate conclusion (12:8).

There then follows the main body of the book (1:12 - 12:7). This consists of four sermons, or discourses. Each one expounds on the two themes of futility and hope. By constant underlining, the overall message of the book becomes too clear to miss. When our outlook is earth-bound ('under the sun'), life is meaningless and hopeless. It has no point. But when we live for the eternal God, it is filled with purpose. There is constant alternation between these two viewpoints, and Solomon faithfully tells us what he observed when he occupied each. However, each section written from the second point of view also contains a good deal of instruction and teaching about the ways of God.

The book then comes to its conclusion (12:8-14), which is little more than a summary of everything that has gone before. If God is not the centre of our existence, life *is* vanity (12:8). The thing to do, then, is to live for him, never forgetting that it is to him that we will finally be answerable (12:9-14).

Key words

Within this clear structure, certain key words crop up repeatedly. Their value is that they help us to recognize which viewpoint Solomon is expressing at any particular point.

The most obvious of these words is 'vanity' or 'futility', which occurs thirty-nine times. This translates a Hebrew word meaning 'something without substance, which quickly passes away'. 'Vanity' is as solid and as enduring as the morning mist. We must constantly call to mind that the modern use of the word, in the sense of empty pride or conceit, was not in Solomon's mind at all. For this reason we shall only use the word 'futility' from this point.

Closely connected with 'futility' is the phrase 'under the

sun', which is found twenty-nine times. It describes the earth-bound and temporal perspective, which sees all of life's activities as pointless. Why not now go quickly through Ecclesiastes, and underline every occurrence of 'futility' and 'under the sun' in black? This simple procedure will go a long way towards helping you identify those passages where Solomon is occupying his first point of view.

Now scan the book again, underlining the word 'God' in red. You will find that it occurs forty times, in small clusters, separated by long passages where he is not mentioned. You have now begun to identify those sections where Solomon occupies his second point of view, brings God into the picture and sees life through the eyes of a converted man.

A fourth key word, which also occurs forty times, is the word 'heart'. This is not closely associated with either one viewpoint or the other, but is worth underlining in a third colour. This will make another point. Unconverted man is in turmoil because of the apparent futility of life. The frustration of it strikes him to the very heart — precisely the place where the converted person senses peace, purpose and fulfilment.

Finally, we should mention the important word 'wisdom' which, with its related words 'wise' and 'wisely', occurs over fifty times. This, too, is not strictly associated with either of Solomon's viewpoints, although two-thirds of its occurrences are in those passages where he is looking at life through the eyes of the unconverted. The exceptions are at 2:26, 12:9 and 11, and in the section 7:1 - 8:13. If these occurrences of the word are underlined in red, and all the others in black, you will have a further indication of which viewpoint Solomon is occupying in any particular passage.

This last key word reminds us that in Ecclesiastes we are reading a very early example of what has been called 'wisdom literature' — a whole species of literature which arose in the ancient Near East from the tenth century B.C. onwards. The pattern which Solomon commenced was followed by many uninspired authors, who set out to give instructions for successful living and to ponder the problems of human existence. They used every possible literary device to make their teaching easy to remember, such as repetition, poetry, comparisons and contrasts, alliteration, riddles, fables and allegories. None of these books would have been penned if Solomon had not led the way by writing Ecclesiastes.

Title

We are now ready to embark on our study of it, but it is possible that there is still one point which is distracting our minds. It concerns the title of the book. 'Ecclesiastes' is a pretty strange name, so how did it originate?

It comes from the opening phrase of the book, 'the words of the Preacher' (1:1). The Hebrew word *qoheleth* designates a person who is the official speaker to an assembly of people. It is not found in any other Old Testament book, but seven times altogether in Ecclesiastes — three times in the first chapter, three times in the last, and once in the middle at 7:27. When the Old Testament was eventually translated into Greek, this word was rendered *ecclesiastes,* and the book became generally known by this name. In English, both the Hebrew and Greek words are translated as 'the Preacher'. Shall we now put ourselves in his congregation, and listen to what he has to say?

2.
The introduction to the book (1:1-11)

Please read Ecclesiastes 1:1-11

1. As the book opens, Solomon identifies himself as the author, without actually naming himself. Who else could possibly have described himself as 'the son of David, king in Jerusalem'? We have before us the words of a man who, because of his privileged position, has sampled all that life has to offer. But he is now king and carries the responsibility of ruling others. He also takes upon himself the responsibility of teaching them and calls himself 'the Preacher'.

2. As he surveys life, Solomon comes to the conclusion that it is all a waste of time. It is pointless. It is meaningless. It has no purpose. Everything about us is temporary, transitory and passing. He underlines this conviction with the Hebrew superlative: 'Futility of futilities . . . futility of futilities; all is futility.'

3. Solomon is, of course, referring to the activities of this earthly life. What is the point of doing all the work that we do, seeing that it eventually comes to nothing? What can a person gain which he will not finally lose? Everything for which we strive, we ultimately forfeit. However much we acquire, in the end we are left with nothing at all.

4. Each man and woman lives for only a short while, and then dies. The earthly stage remains, but different actors are constantly passing across it. In other words, although generations come and go, nothing is ultimately any different.

5-7. There is never any real progress. We live in a world

where there is constant activity, but no actual 'getting anywhere'. Everything goes on as it always has done, but there is no advance. The sun rises and sets, only to rise again. The wind blows and blows, only to come back to where it started. The rivers run into the sea, but never fill it, because the water evaporates and returns to its source. This is the way of the world. The activity never ends, but no destination is ever reached.

8. We are caught up in an endless and wearisome cycle. It is impossible to put into words the futility of it all. The eye sees and sees, and the ear hears and hears, but neither knows what true satisfaction is. Life is inexpressibly monotonous and constantly frustrating.

9. History is as repetitive as nature. It is a ceaseless and tiresome round of activity which never produces anything intrinsically new on this earth.

10-11. If you think you are going to make an indelible mark on the sands of time, you are going to be very disappointed. Any footprints or impressions you make have already been made by others — but the tide has washed them away, just as it will wash away yours, too.

You cannot accomplish anything ultimately worthwhile in this life, and even the memory of your efforts to do so will soon be forgotten. We do not live for long in the reminiscences of others. We must face the facts. Both the world of nature and of human activity are equally futile. They are pointless, purposeless and frustrating. There is no such thing as a lasting accomplishment.

This is life as Solomon saw it from an earth-bound point of view, and this is life as modern philosophers see it. And they are not alone. Countless numbers of ordinary men and women look at life in this way, too. There is no thought which Solomon raises in his introduction, which has not already passed through their minds a thousand times. They live with the constant thought that life is a waste of time. Nothing is worth the effort, for there is nothing which comes to anything in the end.

But is life *really* that pointless? Does it not have *any* meaning? Are our actions *truly* without significance?

If not, what *is* the meaning of life? What sort of life really *is* worthwhile? And how do we go about finding the answer?

These are the questions to which the following chapters will give the answers.

3.
The first sermon   (1:12-3:15)

I   Under the sun (1:12 - 2:23)

    1:12   Intellect

    2:1   Pleasure

    2:12   Pre-eminence   None of these is the key to life

    2:18   Hard work

II   God in the picture (2:24 - 3:15)

    2:24   There is no satisfaction without God

    3:1   Everything is part of a plan

    3:9   Everything is full of purpose

3.
The first sermon   (1:12-3:15)

Please read Ecclesiastes 1:12 - 3:15

In our introduction we pointed out that in this book Solomon alternately surveys life from two perspectives. We now come to see our first example of this. Chapter 1:12 to chapter 3:15 contain the first of the four sermons which constitute the body of the book. If we quickly scan this section, we will find that a great change comes over the sermon at chapter 2:24. Up until then the name of God is mentioned only once. From 2:24 to 3:15 we have a whole cluster of references to him!

1:12 to 2:23 see Solomon surveying life as a man unenlightened by God's revelation. His perspective is earthbound. It is 'under the sun'. But 2:24 to 3:15 see the same man viewing life from God's perspective. We shall call it 'God in the picture'. Let us now discover what conclusions Solomon reached as he surveyed life from these two very different points of view.

I – Under the sun (1:12 - 2:23)

The first eleven verses have already revealed how pointless life appeared to Solomon. He therefore set out to have a closer look at it (12-13). The spirit of enquiry is a God-given faculty, even in an unconverted man. From this earth-bound perspective he came to four conclusions:

1. *1:12-18. Intellect is not the key to life*
At this stage, what Solomon sought more than anything else was knowledge — notice how many times the words 'wisdom' and 'knowledge' come in these verses. But, like

millions of others who have stretched their minds to the limit, he found no lasting satisfaction in this quest. The world remained full of problems that could not be solved, and was empty of so much that could give it meaning and value (15). He came to believe that *all* human activity is a mere 'chasing of the wind', and that it can never lay hold on real fulfilment (14).

Solomon's search took him further than any of his predecessors and he became the wisest man who had ever lived (16). He gave particular attention to the question as to what standard is to be used to decide whether a thing is wise or foolish (17). But then a thought crossed his mind. What is the *point* of such knowledge? Just exactly where have I got to when I have answered that question?

The quest for life's meaning is frustrating, because it is unattainable. When a person gets wiser, and sees that he is no nearer to his goal than before, how much greater is his disappointment! Who can describe his bitterness and grief? (18)

2. 2:1-11. Pleasure is not the key to life

Solomon now turned to self-indulgence as a possible source of complete satisfaction. He did not blindly grasp at life's pleasures, but conducted his search with thoroughness and care — which is the meaning of verse 3. Indeed, for a moment his exploits brought him some measure of happiness. He felt a short-lived sense of accomplishment (10b). Yet when he stopped to take stock of the real results, he was forced to admit that the path of pleasure had not brought him any permanent gain. *This* was not the path to enduring satisfaction (11).

What pleasures did he try? His whole time was spent seeking something new. He travelled the highway of new experiences — mirth, enjoyment, laughter, drunkenness, wisdom and folly (1-3). He amassed to himself ever new and more extravagant possessions — houses, vineyards gardens, orchards, pools, servants, unsurpassed property, silver and gold, royal treasure (works of art?), choirs and every other imaginable sort of gratification, including every kind of musical instrument (4-8). So very many who walk the path of self-indulgence can only dream of what they would like to have. Solomon suffered from no such limitation. His greatness permitted him to have his every whim, and to possess everything he had ever set his eye on (9-10).

The pursuit of pleasure did not mean that he had turned his back on the use of his intellect (9b). But even a combination of keys does not unlock the meaning of life and give it enduring satisfaction. None of his experiences or possessions could rid him of the conviction that all his quests were a waste of time, resulting in no lasting gain. The paths of intellect and pleasure had not taken him off the path of futility (11).

3. *2:12-17. Pre-eminence is not the key to life*
Solomon knew that he excelled most men in virtually every area of life. His successor might possibly equal him, but would never surpass him.

As he looked at the world, he could see in it wisdom (such as he himself had), as well as madness and folly (12a). He could see that one is infinitely superior to the other (13). After all, a wise man can see what is ahead and chooses his way accordingly. In this way he avoids unnecessary suffering and brings himself a good deal of happiness. By contrast, a foolish person merely gropes his way through life and his happiness comes to him more by chance (14a). It is not difficult to see which of these two paths is preferable.

But the advantage which the wise person has does not last for long (14b). Both wise and foolish end up at the same destination. What, then, is the point of trying to be 'top man'? The 'rat-race' is utter folly! (15) The wise do not even live on in the memories of others more than do the foolish. However different their lives may have been, both soon die and are quickly forgotten (16).

This discovery filled Solomon with bitterness (17). All that he had worked for was pointless. All his efforts were ultimately a waste of time. Those pre-eminent in this life, for whatever reason, have no lasting advantage. Everything that we do is futility. It is a chasing after wind! (17b)

4. *2:18-23. Hard work is not the key to life*

Eight times the word 'labour' occurs in this section. Solomon did not spend all his time pursuing wisdom, indulging himself, or seeking pre-eminence. He also kept building, investing and producing. But even the thought of this was sour (18a). What was the point of it all? Everything we gain we leave to someone else — and who knows what sort of person *that* will be? (18b-19)

As he trod the path of hard work Solomon stopped, turned round and took a long hard look at the way he had come. What he saw filled him with despair. Had all the effort and discomfort been worth it? (20)

When life draws to its close, what have we got out of working so hard? We think, and work, and plan, and use our minds — all to leave what we have gained to someone else who, as likely as not, will not deserve it. He certainly will not have worked for it, and will therefore probably not value it, but squander it (21). A man may work and worry all his life, but at the end of the day, what good does it do him? He worries, he travails, he loses sleep — and all for what? (22)

What *is* the point of it all? Where *is* lasting satisfaction to be found? It is not in a high level of education, with a string of letters after my name and a reputation for being learned. It is not in having my every material desire supplied. It is not in my arriving at the top rung of my particular ladder. Nor is there even a lasting sense of fulfilment in having worked hard all my life. None of these things, in

the long run, turns out to be worthwhile. What *is* the life
worth living?

There is neither point nor purpose in chasing after the
four things which have been mentioned. Is there such a
thing as a life *with* point, *with* purpose? The answer now
comes to us in the second half of this first sermon.

II – God in the picture (2:24 - 3:15)

There *is* purpose in life, if God is in the picture – this is
the central lesson of what follows. Now seeing life from the
perspective of a person whose mind has been enlightened
by God's revelation, Solomon comes to three conclusions
– conclusions which are radically different from those he
had reached previously.

1. *2:24-26. There is no satisfaction without God*
He is now able to see that true satisfaction *is* possible,
but that we do not have the power to bestow it upon ourselves. It is something given – given by God. Notice how
many times the word 'give' occurs in verse 26.

Leupold's translation of verses 24 and 25 brings out the
same point: 'It is not a good thing *inherent* in man that he
is able to eat and drink and get satisfaction in his toil.
This, too, have I seen that such a thing is entirely from the
hand of God. For who can eat, and who can have enjoyment apart from Him?'

To the person with whom he is pleased, God gives wisdom, knowledge and joy (26a). It is the sinner – the
person who leaves God out of the reckoning and goes
against him – who lives a life of futility and spends his
days chasing the wind (26b). Everything which the sinner
does, however, ultimately works out for the benefit of
those who are in God's favour (26, middle).

Solomon is quite clear: life immediately takes on some

meaning and purpose once God is brought into the picture.
Precisely how this comes about will be amplified as the
book proceeds.

2. 3:1-8. *Everything is part of a plan*

What follows is the best known passage in Ecclesiastes,
although it ought to be said that thousands of those who
have some acquaintance with these verses are quite un-
aware that they are found in the Bible. The passage consists of pairs of contrasts, all of which are total opposites.
Each pair is introduced by the words 'a time' — an expression which, in the original language, refers to an occurrence
which is predetermined. The first pair, 'a time to be born,
and a time to die' (2a), introduces all the rest, for all the
others take place between these two events.

But what is the purpose of this section? Why is it included, and what is it intended to teach?

From his earth-bound perspective Solomon had con-
cluded that everything in this life is without significance.
But now, as he looks at life from God's point of view, he
sees that that is not the way things are at all!

Everything in this universe is part of a grand scheme (1).
There is a season, an appointed period, for *every* event. All
that takes place occurs at its appropriate time. It has been
predetermined. Every detail of life serves an overall purpose, and plays its part in bringing that purpose to pass.
Seemingly chance events are all tied in to an eternal
plan.

When a man has this perspective, how different he is!
While the unconverted continue to ask, 'What is the point
of it all?' he sees that there is a point in *everything*. This is
the foundation for the believer's comfort that all things
work together for his good. Even his or her own calling to be
a believing man or woman is part of an eternal purpose
(Romans 8:28).

3. *3:9-15. Everything is full of purpose*

The unconverted person cannot help asking questions
about life. Sometimes he puts his question in the form
in which it is found in verse 9. 'At the end of the day,
what does a worker get out of all his toil?' he asks. It is
God himself who moves men and women to such question-
ing, and causes them to be in perplexity (10).

The answer is that everything in life is of significance,
and is in its right and appropriate place in the overall plan.
It is therefore beautiful (11a). Man looks beyond everyday
occurrences and asks the meaning of them all. This is
because he is a spiritual creature. Eternity is in his heart (a
point which modern translations bring out well in their
treatment of this verse), and it is natural to him to ask ultimate questions (11b). He has reasoning power, and gives
himself to analysing the whole sweep of life. But, unaided,
he never comes up with the right answer. He is totally
unable to see exactly what God is doing, and which way he
is taking (11c).

The best thing a person can do, therefore, is to come to
terms with this limitation, to rejoice in God's gifts to him,
to do good and to enjoy the passing blessings of his labour
– accepting them as God's gifts (12-13).

What *we* do soon passes. What God does is for ever. It is
never imperfect or defective. God is working out his plan
in all events everywhere, and his purpose in doing so is that
we should fear him (14).

And so the apparently endless cycle goes on (15). But it
is *not* without significance. It is *God* who brings to pass
again what has previously taken place and disappeared. *He*
operates the cycle, and causes what has always gone on to
reoccur. That being so, we cannot possibly argue that it is
purposeless. It serves his purpose, and is all under his direction. Nothing then, anywhere, is pointless.

These are lessons which Ecclesiastes intends us to take
to heart. They are of particular value in this modern age,

where so many of us are called to perform tasks which
are monotonous, repetitive and of no obvious value. Our
industrial society is organized in such a way that we easily
come to think of ourselves as entirely insignificant cogs in
a vast and impersonal machine. Neither we nor our tasks
seem to matter. But once we recognize that there is a God,
and that everything is in his hand, then *everything* takes on
meaning and significance. The moment we forget this,
everything in life appears to be pointless — sheer futility.

Every man and woman on earth is faced with two clear
alternatives. He must either live a life of measureless
frustration, or he must live his life in the fear of God.

4.
The second sermon   (3:16-5:20)

I   Futility (3:16 - 4:16)

    3:16 No pre-eminence
    4:1   No comforter
    4:4   No rest
    4:7   No companion
    4:13 No following

II   Worship of God (5:1-7)

    5:1   House of God
    5:4   Vows to God

III Futility (5:8-17)

    5:8   No justice
    5:10 No satisfaction
    5:13 No permanence

IV   Gifts from God (5:18-20)

4.
The second sermon (3:16-5:20)

Please read Ecclesiastes 3:16 - 5:20

Solomon's second sermon is basically the same as his first. In the first sermon he occupied each viewpoint only once. If we quickly scan the section before us, and notice the paragraphs where God's name is entirely absent and the paragraphs where his name occurs in clusters, we shall see that this time he occupies each viewpoint twice. His starting-point is the same as before, and so is his finish, but he also alternates between the two viewpoints in between.

The lessons are the same as before, also. To the person with an earth-bound view, life is futile. There is no other word for it. There is frankly no meaning to life unless one has a personal relationship with God. All that is really new about this sermon is the way in which these now familiar truths are illustrated and applied.

I – Futility (3:16 - 4:16)

1. *3:16-22. No pre-eminence*
In his quest, conducted from the earth-bound point of view, Solomon now looked into the courts of law (16). It is here that one might expect to find a proper administration of justice. But all he discovered instead was wickedness and iniquity. In the place of supposed righteousness there was a rejection of moral values.

'How can they get away with it?' he asked; and then through his mind passed the suggestion that God must

32

have appointed a future judgement when he will right all the wrongs which have been committed. Surely wickedness cannot go unpunished for ever! There *must* be a time — some time — when an account will have to be rendered for every thought and deed.

But then into Solomon's unenlightened mind came a contradictory thought. 'Perhaps what is going on is rather different,' it said. 'Perhaps God is permitting all this injustice to demonstrate to men and women that, despite their intelligence, they are really no different from the animals (18). After all, in the end they *are* no different. They die and return to the dust, just like animals do (19-20). They all go to the same place. And who knows whether what happens to men after death is any different from what happens to other creatures? (21) Nobody has any proof one way or the other, so who knows for sure? There is nothing in man to show that he is any different.'

'In the light of this, a person ought to concentrate on making the best of this life that he can (22). You cannot be *certain* that there is anything to follow. Who is going to enable you to enjoy anything after you have gone?'

2. 4:1-3. No comforter
And yet the possibility of enjoying this life is really rather slim. Life is full of oppression. Power is on the side of the oppressors. The oppressed cry, but there is nobody to take their side. Their tears flow, but there is no comforter (1).

Because there is so much oppression, the only happy people are those who are dead. So much for Solomon's self-advice to do your best to enjoy this life! Indeed, he concludes that the happiest and most blessed of all are those who have never been born (2-3).

3. 4:4-6. No rest
But Solomon *had* been born, and he continued to look at life around him. In looking at human toil and skill he con-

cluded that it was entirely futile – because although a man may achieve something in this life, what motivates him is 'keeping up with the Joneses', an unworthy envy of his neighbour. On the other hand, the person who does *not* work destroys himself, for you cannot live on nothing (4-5). The metaphorical expression at the end of verse 5 means that the person who does not work uses up all his resources until he has nothing left to feed upon except *himself*!

However, the opposite extreme is just as bad. Work undoubtedly brings some reward, but too much of it brings nothing but trouble. It is better to have modest earnings and a restful mind than to make large gains, with their accompanying anxiety (6).

Who can count how many over-ambitious executives have learned the truth of these words, without ever reading them here? And who among us does not know a score of wives who look back with longing to the days when their now successful husbands had less responsibilities, less anxieties and less money – but more time to enjoy what really matters in this life. Those were days of an almost infinitely greater peace of mind, which stand in stark contrast to their present dissatisfied restlessness.

4. *4:7-12. No companion*

It is a fact of life that wealth often makes a man a miser, so that he withdraws from the company of others. The picture of verse 8 is of a man who is so caught up with avarice that he chooses to work alone, rather than to share his profits with anyone. Without partner or helper he gives himself to amassing wealth – wealth which he will be unable to leave to anyone, for he will have no one to leave it to!

What futility! Ever working, yet never satisfied, such a man never stops to ask what the point is in gathering so much wealth (7-8). His life-style deprives him of one of the few joys this world has to offer — companionship. There are such blessings in having friends. You accomplish more, have help available when in distress, and enjoy warmth, protection and security (9-12a). If fellowship with two is that good, how much better is fellowship with three! A cord with three strands is considerably stronger than one with only two (12b).

5. 4:13-16. No following

But some do not spend their days in such lonely wealth-seeking. Popularity is their goal. Never has this been more true than during these last years of the twentieth century. It is astonishing that Solomon was able to write such relevant words so long ago! His estimate of those who seek popularity is entirely up to date. Those who seek the acclaim of others will never find any real satisfaction. This is because popularity depends on the fickleness of people. It is far too insecure a foundation on which to build lasting happiness.

To illustrate this, Solomon considers the hypothetical example of a poor youth who has succeeded in becoming king (13). After years in the public eye, he is now an old man blinded to his limitations and his need of wise counsel. Solomon considers that he was better off as the poor youth that he used to be. At least in those days he was open to learning. In the area of teachability his age and experience have taught him nothing.

It was from prison that this man came to the throne, unseating the then occupant in doing so (14). But, writes Solomon, 'I have seen all the living under the sun throng to the side of the second lad who replaces him' (15, NASB). In other words, the old king has entirely failed to realize that popular favour is uncertain and unpredictable. Public opinion is as ready to back a young man planning to replace him, as it was to support him in his own rise to power.

People will dethrone anybody in order to get what they

want. Popular acclaim is a fickle and transient commodity. Indeed, when the new contender is enthroned there will be those who will not be happy with him, who will be ready to support someone else (16). There is no end to the people who have walked this path — raised to the heights, then cast to the depths, by the shallow wishes of others. No one is a hero for long. Anyone seeking satisfaction by seeking popularity is chasing the wind (16b).

This first section of the sermon has given us a vivid picture of the hopelessness of unconverted men and women. They try to enjoy this life, because they are so deeply uncertain of the next. But in this life they are exposed to oppression, and to the wide extremes of either starvation through poverty or anxiety caused by wealth. It is possible to become so engrossed in the search for wealth that one goes through life lonely; or to be borne along on the waves of popularity one moment, only to be drowned in the waves of forgetfulness and disappointment the next.

From his earth-bound perspective Solomon has come to the same conclusion as last time. Nothing in this life is ultimately worthwhile. Whatever you put your mind to is, in fact, a waste of time. It is pointless.

II — Worship of God (5:1-7)

At chapter 5:1 Solomon's viewpoint dramatically changes, and we come to a short section liberally sprinkled with references to God.

There seems to be no connection between this verse and what has just gone before, and no doubt this is deliberate. When we enter into the mind of someone surveying life from the divine standpoint, we are in a different world. Their thoughts, compared with those of the unconverted, could not be more different. While unregenerate people trouble their minds concerning the futility and frustrations of this life, the spiritual person is meditating on higher themes. In this section Solomon is considering the subject of the worship of God, and what should be remembered when paying vows to him. The thoughts of the unconverted are dominated by money and enjoyment, because that is what they live for. But the spiritual person lives for God, and is most at home when God is in his thoughts.

1. *5:1-3. House of God*
Solomon is thinking about what advice to give in the subject of proper worship. It is that we should guard our steps when we go into the house of God. In other words, the worshipper should enter thoughtfully and cautiously, fully aware of what he is doing (1).

In his phrase, 'Be more ready to hear,' Solomon is not speaking of coming to the temple to hear the exposition of Scripture, but is continuing to caution us against approaching the worship of God in the wrong way. Foolish minds think that God may be worshipped just as *they* please, but that is not the case. We should worship him as *he* himself has specified, and should remember that not to do so is sin.

We need to ask whether our own generation takes such teaching seriously. There is now hardly a church anywhere which has not imported into its worship some element which is not specifically approved by God's Word.

In our worship we should not be in a hurry to speak. We should solemnly recall the enormity of what we are doing. God is in *heaven*. We are nothing more than creatures on earth. When we remember this, we will quickly see that there is no merit in pouring out words of worship. A few sincere words are much more in keeping (2).

Solomon then quotes an ancient proverb to support this advice (3). Just as a night of dreams is the inevitable outcome of getting too engrossed in business, so nonsensical speech is the result of saying too much at worship.

2. 5:4-7. Vows to God

From worship he moves to the subject of vows. I am making a vow to God when I promise him something which his law does not require of me. Every vow is voluntary, but this does not mean that they may be taken lightly. When we make vows, we are to *do* what we have promised — otherwise it is better not to vow at all (4-5).

'Do not let your mouth lead you into sin,' counsels Solomon (6), 'nor say to the priest on duty, "It was a mistake." Why make God unnecessarily angry?'

The word 'flesh' in verse 6 is a Hebrew way of referring to the whole person. Why let a sin of one part of the body — the mouth — cause the whole of oneself to be in trouble with God?

In verse 7 Solomon is alluding back to verse 3, and summing up his point. Just as too much concern over business brings too many dreams, so too many words spoken at worship bring rash promises, and therefore judgement from God. Only a proper fear of God will prevent a person falling into this error and its appalling consequence. Is this something we are doing our best to cultivate?

III — Futility (5:8-17)

Learning how to fear God properly is what interests a spiritual person most. But, as we saw from the previous 'earth-bound' section, the unspiritual person is occupied with himself, and very especially with the theme of making himself rich. Solomon now returns to this perspective and, to continue showing us its utter futility, he now writes three paragraphs about hopeless situations involving money.

1. 5:8-9. No justice

Solomon notices that societies are organized as hierarchies.

The source of all wealth is the ground, where all plants and crops grow, and where minerals and all other natural resources are to be found. But the person who works the ground has somebody over him. He in turn has somebody over him, and so it goes on, all the way up to the king. The ground feeds and supplies them all, even the king himself. But each person on the ladder uses the person beneath him to his own advantage. He could not enjoy what he enjoys if that person were not there. His personal interest is best served by keeping the hierarchical ladder intact, no matter what means are employed to do so. This being so, do not be surprised when you see men oppressing and exploiting others. How else can they preserve their comfortable position? There can never be justice where there is greed.

2. *5:10-12. No satisfaction*
But greedy people need reminding that the actual possession of wealth never brings satisfaction. Greed and contentment are opposites. The wealth-loving person never feels that he has enough. He always wants more (10).

Yet the simple fact is that as your goods increase, so do your liabilities. The more you have, the more material demands are made upon you. What advantage, then, is there in getting rich — except that of feasting your eyes on a larger turnover? You may not *have* more, but you do *handle* more (11).

As for the man who has worked for what he owns, at least he sleeps well, whether his wealth is small or great. But that is not the case with the rich person. The numberless anxieties which riches bring crowd in upon him and keep him awake! (12)

3. *5:13-17. No permanence*
What insecure possessions riches are! The futility and folly of setting your heart upon them is obvious. For instance, a man may accumulate a fortune, only to lose it all in one

unfortunate business deal, leaving him nothing to pass on to his son (13-14).

In any event, you cannot take *any* of it with you when you go. *Nobody* leaves the world richer than when he came in. So what is the point in living for riches? What profit can we finally make? At the end of your life you have got nothing out of it (15-16).

Not only so, but your mortal years of wealth are years filled with such troubles as sorrow, anger and sickness. However rich you are, your wealth cannot immunize you against such contingencies, while they themselves prevent you from enjoying fully all the things that you own (17). You are as likely to find satisfaction in material prosperity as you are to grasp the wind! (16b)

IV – Gifts from God (5:18-20)

Whatever he may call the path which he walks, no unconverted person has yet succeeded in taking himself off the path of futility. Even the richest among them is bankrupt. How very different is the person who lives for God! The brief closing paragraph of Solomon's sermon, written from the spiritual point of view, most powerfully underlines the contrast.

He does not see the blessings of this life simply as the fruit of his own labour – but as gifts from *God*! Food, drink, all good things, life, riches, wealth, our various faculties, the power to rejoice, gladness of heart – all these things come from God's hand. The godly person reasons that God has given him these things that he might enjoy them, and he is able to do so because he sees them all as symbols and pledges of God's favour (18-19).

No doubt the believer, like other men and women, has his fair share of difficulties. But he does not get totally absorbed by them, because he has these other things to think about. Seeing life's good things as signs of God's favour, his heart is set alight with rejoicing, and filled with godly joy (20). He thinks life is *good,* and knows what it is to have a heart bursting with happiness.

It was his possessions and the experiences of this life which caused unbearable frustration in the heart of the unbeliever in the 'earth-bound' sections of this second sermon. The very same things stir the spirit of the believer to gladness and delight. 'Life is not worth living, apart from redemption,' said Oswald Chambers in summing up the message of Ecclesiastes, and in doing so he perfectly captured the essence of this sermon.

Unless God is in the picture, a person's predicament is hopeless. But once he is seen as the Giver of every good thing in life, the recipient will not only want to rejoice in his gifts, but to worship and serve him. The teaching on worship and vows found in the middle of this section is now seen to be most appropriate and relevant.

5.
The third sermon   (6:1-8:13)

I   Futility — three things which are a waste of time
     (6:1-12)

     6:1   Hoping wealth will last
     6:3   Hoping wealth will satisfy
     6:10   Hoping things will change

II   Wisdom — nine things which are worthwhile
     (7:1 - 8:13)

     7:1   Honour is better than luxury
     7:2   Seriousness is better than frivolity
     7:7   Restraint is better than rashness
     7:11   Wisdom is better than wealth
     7:13   Submission is better than rebellion
     7:15   Godliness is better than anything
     7:23   Revelation is better than reason
     8:1   Discretion is better than stubbornness
     8:6   The fear of God is better than evil

5.
The third sermon (6:1-8:13)

Please read Ecclesiastes 6:1 - 8:13

Solomon's third sermon follows the general pattern of the previous two. First of all, he occupies the position of an unenlightened person and speaks about the problem of futility (ch.6). Then, from the viewpoint of someone in fellowship with God, he gives the solution (7:1 - 8:13).

The first section asks, 'Who knows what is good for a man in this life?' (6:12) The second section replies, 'The truly wise person knows . . .' (8:5). On this occasion the spiritual viewpoint contains several references to God, but is more characterized by clusters of godly words, especially 'wise', 'wisdom' and related words, and 'fear'. Because the last paragraph (8:6-13) contains none of these words, many Bible students consider it as the beginning of a new unit of thought. This may be so, but we will see that it also links coherently and naturally with the material immediately before it, and can legitimately be considered as the closing paragraph of the third sermon.

We come, then, to learn the same lessons as before. The approach is different, but not the conclusions reached. The meaning of some of the details may escape us, but the central thrust of the whole sermon is powerfully direct.

I – Futility – three things which are a waste of time (6:1-12)

1. *6:1-2. Hoping wealth will last*
Once more Solomon surveys life as an unconverted person

would, and reasons that one of life's greatest misfortunes
(1) is that a man who has all the riches that his heart could
wish for is not able to enjoy them.

This is because he dies early, before he is able to consider
doing so. He has no son to be his heir, so instead a stranger
inherits everything. What a waste of time it was amassing
all that wealth! What a human tragedy — to have spent all
that time building up an empire of luxury and wealth, and
never to have enjoyed it! And, of course, this is not something which only happened years ago. How many times
have we seen it happen ourselves!

2. 6:3-9. Hoping wealth will satisfy

But let us take a completely opposite case. Let us imagine
a man who lives long enough to father a hundred children.
This is no guarantee that he will enjoy life. Indeed, were he
to live for ever, and still not be able to enjoy life, it would
have been better if he had not lived at all (3). The baby
born as a result of a miscarriage — who comes and goes
almost without mention, who never sees the light of day,
and so never has any of life's experiences — that baby is
better off than he is (3b-5).

Should a person live for two thousand years, he only
ends up where that miscarriage has gone (6). He spends all
his days feeding his mouth, and yet is never satisfied (7).
We must face the facts. In the end, the wise person is no
better off than the fool, and the person who is poor gains
nothing by learning how to conduct himself before others.
Nobody is ultimately better off than anybody else, or
secures any lasting advantage (8).

How much better it is to be content with what you have
than to spend life with longings that can never be satisfied!
(9a) But that is never the way it is, as Solomon has already
told us, and as our own experience has also taught us.
People never seem to learn from the experience of previous
generations, and continue to look on wealth as the road to

satisfaction. Their hopes are always disappointed. The path
leads nowhere. Grasping satisfaction is as elusive as clutch-
ing the wind (9b).

3. *6:10-12. Hoping things will change*
So life goes on as it has always gone on. There is never anything new. Death remains mankind's undefeatable foe. No
one can contend with him and win (10). And so it is that
every person's efforts to find lasting satisfaction in this life
end up in frustration (11). Who knows where the life
worth living is to be found? Life is so transitory, so lacking
in substance and so soon gone. And who knows what will
happen when it is all over? (12) Unenlightened man, looking at life from an earth-bound perspective, has plenty of
questions — but no real answers . . .

Proof that things have not changed is seen in the fact
that this chapter, written so long ago, is a perfect description of modern man's problem, too. Never has he had so
many *things*. But they do not satisfy him. This is clear
from the way that he expects the very latest invention to
please him in a way that his existing possessions cannot.
But he knows that whatever he comes to own, or to try, it
will soon be gone. Not only so, but he himself will soon be
gone, too — and who knows what will follow? Where *is*
enduring satisfaction to be found?

It is with unconverted man's problem so vividly painted
before us that Solomon now speaks again. His point of
view is now that of a person enlightened by God's revelation. However, this time he does things a little differently.
Previously he has come straight in, and has declared that
life only has purpose if God is in the picture and if we
know, worship and serve Him. This time the approach is to
show us that in this life some things are better than others.
Not everything is of equal value. He uses that point eventually to demonstrate that in this world there are different

sorts of life which go on side by side. Rubbing shoulders with the wicked are those who fear God and, in the end, their sort of life is *better*.

II — Wisdom — nine things which are worthwhile (7:1 - 8:13)

1. *7:1. Honour is better than luxury*
The first item on Solomon's list is the assertion that having a good reputation is better than enjoying the luxury of fine perfume — a real status symbol in the ancient East. When a person is born you can only measure his life in terms of its potential. When he dies, you can look back on what he has actually accomplished. How much better to go out of life having accomplished something worthwhile, than to have passed your days in meaningless self-indulgence!

2. *7:2-6. Seriousness is better than frivolity*
Here is a paragraph of particular relevance to our entertainment-crazed generation, with the endless banter of its paid comedians, the cult-worship of its pop stars and its general adulation of all that is trivial.

Both seriousness and frivolity are found in the world, but one is better than the other. For instance, when a person visits a house in mourning, he *learns* something — that life is brief and death certain. He takes this to heart and sees the need to live wisely. This is not a lesson which a person is very likely to learn at a party (2).

It is better to be thoughtful and serious about the problems of life than to laugh them off. It is a course of action which is much more likely to help the heart (3). A common example can be found in the sense of relief which a sad person experiences after giving vent to his or her feelings in weeping.

A fool can think only about laughter, but a wise person constantly remembers that death is a fact, and takes

account of it in forming his life-view (4). The serious talk
of such a person is infinitely better than the songs of those
who try to sing themselves out of thinking deeply about
life's issues. It is better to have your sins pointed out than
to be entertained! (5) A fool's talk may make a great noise.
The impression may be good. But it accomplishes nothing
— just as thorn bushes crackle on the fire, but do not gener-
ate sufficient heat to boil the pot. They are worthless (6).

3. 7:7-10. Restraint is better than rashness
Restraint and rashness are found side by side in this world,
too. But that is not to say that they are of equal worth.
The point of this paragraph is to remind us that a person
needs to keep himself in check, for there are all sorts of
influences which can pervert his heart and can cause him
to act out of character. Extortion can turn the wisest of
men into a fool, and everyone knows how corrupting
bribery is (7).

It is sensible to be cautious in your speech, since it is
only after you have spoken that you will be in a position
to work out what the full effect of your words has been
(8). Do not, therefore, be in a hurry to give expression to
your anger, lest you end up by saying something that you
may regret. Only fools are quick-tempered (9).

We must always think about what we are going to say
before we open our mouths. It is much better to take a
quiet second look at the past and present before pronounc-
ing that things were better years ago (10). It is perfectly
possible that over the years we have forgotten many of the
difficulties and disadvantages of those times, and if we
speak unguardedly we shall certainly not speak very wisely.

4. 7:11-12. Wisdom is better than wealth
The qualities considered in the previous two paragraphs are
opposites. If you have one, you cannot have the other. But
not everything is like that. Take wisdom and wealth, for

example. It is possible to have *both* of them in this world and, if you do, you are rich indeed! (11) What an excellent combination they are! Both provide some measure of protection (12a), but do not think that they are therefore equals. Wealth can provide you with so many of the good things which this world has to offer. Wisdom is superior, because it gives *life* to those who have it (12b). 'Life' in Ecclesiastes means that life which is worth living, which is the privilege of those who live and die in the fear of God. This is something which wealth can never purchase. Only wisdom knows the way to it.

5. 7:13-14. Submission is better than rebellion

What we must remember is that our lives are in the hand of God, and are ordered by him. We cannot make things different from the way he has shaped them (13). Both our days of prosperity and our days of adversity are determined by him. By all means rejoice in the former, but do not be conquered by the spirit of rebellion when you experience the second. Stop and consider! *Both* are from him − one as much as the other. You simply do not know which will come to you next (14). It is impossible for you to unveil what the future holds, and in this way you are reminded of your own creatureliness. The best thing to do is this: take each day, whatever it holds, as from *him*!

6. 7:15-22. Godliness is better than everything

Solomon is now beginning to approach the point that he really wants us to get to. In this life all sorts of qualities, experiences and lives run side by side. But he has established that some of them are better than others. Yet there is something better than them all. It is godliness.

Solomon tells us that even when he viewed life as an earth-bound man, he noticed that the righteous do not necessarily live either longer or more happily than the wicked (15). Indeed, it is a common sight to see the wicked outliving the righteous. It occurred to him that if 'the good die young', it was sensible not to be too righteous and wise, in case his life should be cut short (16). On the other hand, it was just as important to avoid the opposite extreme of unashamed wickedness, because God might possibly step in in judgement, and cut short his life for a different reason (17).

So much for the advice of his unconverted days! Now his tune has changed, and he invites us to get hold of something, and to get hold of it properly (18a). Instead of walking a tightrope of trying to avoid too much righteousness on one side and too much wickedness on the other, give yourself to the fear of God. The person who does that comes off best of all (18b).

Such wisdom gives a person power (19), but it does not make him perfect (20). Therefore do not be too sensitive to criticism, and go about trying to hear what people are saying about you. If you do that, it will not be too long before you hear something you would have preferred *not* to hear (21). When you *do* hear such criticism, however, do not lay it too much to heart. Remember the thoughts which have gone through your mind about others (22).

7. 7:23-29. Revelation is better than reason

In this comparing of one thing with another, and his concluding which are better, Solomon tells us that the lessons he has been passing on have been tested and proved in the arena of everyday living. He is not giving us a catalogue of theoretical speculation, but wisdom which has been *demonstrated* to be wise (23a).

He then tells us about his own search for wisdom. He tried to be wise through self-effort, but got nowhere (23b-24). Wisdom was quite simply out of reach. He made every effort to discover what it is, and also tried to define what it is that makes certain courses of action to be folly and stupidity (25).

One thing he learned in his search — there is nothing in this life as bad or as dangerous as a wicked woman (26). How many people are irretrievably ensnared by her! Those who enjoy God's favour will escape her, but never those who love their sin.

But adding together all that he had learned in his search, Solomon still found himself unable to unravel the mysteries of life (27-28a). Wisdom is all but absent from the human race. Very, very occasionally one stumbles across a truly wise man, but never across a wise woman (28).

'But this I know,' concludes Solomon, 'God originally made mankind different. He was made upright, but has since pursued many purposes and schemes which have brought wickedness into the world' (29). That is *all* that man's unaided reason has succeeded in doing. Reason, unenlightened by revelation, has brought nothing but ruin.

8. 8:1-5. Discretion is bettter than stubbornness

As for the wise man — so very rare — he has no equal, no peer. Only he knows the meaning of life, and the explanation of things. Such wisdom brings its own joy, and this is reflected in the way that his stern features are replaced by a bright and beaming face (1).

At this point Solomon presses upon his readers a particular example of wisdom. Writing as a king, he gives advice concerning relationships with kings. Obey him, he counsels, remembering how you took an oath before God to do so (2). Do not be in a hurry to leave his presence. Do not stand up for a cause which he is unlikely to approve (3). Remember, he is the *king,* and it is *his* will that will be done, and not yours. He will do exactly as he pleases, so it is pointless to champion a cause which is contrary to his wishes. His word prevails and he is answerable to nobody (4).

No evil will come your way if you behave like this before him. There is a proper time and procedure for everything,

as every wise heart well knows (5). This principle still holds
good, although none of us now lives under the sort of mon-
archy which Solomon had in mind as he wrote this section.

9. *8:6-13. The fear of God is better than evil*
It is this fact, that there is a time for everything and a way
for it to be done, which is the cause of man's predicament
(6). He simply does not know what the future holds, so
how can he know *when* future events will come to pass?
(7) But he does know that there is one certainty from which
he cannot be released. Not even the deviousness of the
wicked can secure for them an escape. It is the fact of
death (8).

Of all the problems that a person faces in this life, death
is the supreme one, observes Solomon. We can exercise our
minds in other areas — for instance, on how one man can
dominate another, and merely succeed in ruining himself
in the process (9). But there is one fact we cannot miss.
The wicked end up by being buried. They may keep up an
appearance of religion, and even receive praise for their
exploits. But they end up dead, buried and forgotten, in
the very city where they did their crimes. What a waste of
time such living is! How pointless! (10)

Why, then, do people commit themselves to lives of
wickedness? The answer is straightforward. It is because
their sins are not punished *at once* that they do it (11).
But although such a person may commit a hundred crimes,
and live for an exceptionally long time, we must not think
that he is better off than the godly person (12). In fact,
the opposite is true. The person who fears God will be
better off in the long run. It is to such people that the
ultimate benefits belong. However long the evil person
who does not fear God may live, he will not live for ever.
Things appear to go well for him at the moment, but his
shadow will not lengthen indefinitely. One day the sun will
go down for him, too (12b-13).

Can we see how Solomon has reached his conclusion? He has displayed that in this world there is such a thing as better and worse. Some courses of action are preferable to others.

In his consideration of opposites Solomon has included ungodliness and godliness. These different sorts of living, found side by side in this world, are not equal options. When the ungodly person dies, he is left with nothing. All he has ever lived for, he has left behind — and he *still* has the great fact of God to face. Meanwhile the spiritual person has lived in quite a distinct manner in this world. There is a certain quality about him, as we have seen. It is true that he dies, too, but when he does so he *still* has all that he ever lived for — God! It is this fact which reveals why the godly life must be classified as the better, and the evil one as the worse. But this is not simply a fact which we should grasp. It is a truth which should govern all our living.

6.
The fourth sermon   (8:14-12:7)

I   Futility (8:14 - 10:20)

    8:14 - 9:16 Enjoy yourself while you can

        8:15-17   Because God's purposes are unknowable
        9:1-10   Because death is the end
        9:11-16   Because life is uncertain

    9:17 - 10:20 Lessons worth learning

        9:17 - 10:15 About wisdom and folly
          9:17-18; 10:12-14 — wise use of words
          10:2-4, 8-11   — wise conduct
          10:1, 5-7, 15   — wisdom compared with folly
        10:16-20   About the rule of kings

II   Purpose (11:1 - 12:7)

    11:1-8 Do good whenever you can
    11:9 - 12:7 Serve God while you are young

6.
The fourth sermon (8:14-12:7)

Please read Ecclesiastes 8:14 - 12:7

The pattern of Solomon's fourth sermon does not alter appreciably from the three which have preceded it. For over two and a half chapters he occupies the position of an unconverted man, drawing unenlightened conclusions about life (8:14 - 10:20), before speaking for one and a half chapters as a person in fellowship with God (11:1 - 12:7).

However, more than any of the previous sermons, this one draws out how very different are these two sorts of people. Both of them look at life and consider death. But their reflections are in sharp contrast to each other. Their two sets of priorities have nothing in common and they are led into totally contradictory life-styles.

I – Futility (8:14 - 10:20)

1. *8:14 - 9:16. Enjoy yourself while you can*
a. *Because God's purposes are unknowable (8:15-17)*
There can be few passages, even in God's Word, which throw more light than this one on just how an unconverted person thinks. As Solomon surveys life and enquires what sort of life is worth living, he concludes that the best a person can do is to enjoy himself while he can. Life is unpredictable. You just do not know what is going to happen to whom. We frequently observe that righteous people

receive what the wicked deserve and vice versa (14). So while you can you should 'have a good time'. Eat, drink and be merry. Such pleasures are tangible things which you can lay hold of (15), whereas, try as you might, you can never find out the meaning of life (16-17). What is the point of it all — especially of all our hard work? Not even the wisest of men knows the answer, despite his claim to do so.

b. Because death is the end (9:1-10)
All sorts of people are running life's race. But there is no telling which of them are pleasing God and which are not. Nobody knows whether his deeds are earning God's love or calling down his hatred (1). In any case, whichever way we live, we all come to the same end. We share a common destiny — the grave! (2-3)

It is better to be alive than dead (4). You are conscious. You *are* somebody. You get something out of living. But the dead know nothing, gain nothing and are forgotten (5). Whether they were good or bad no longer matters. They are gone. Never again will they share in all that takes place under the sun (6).

So live life while you can. Enjoy what you can enjoy — food, drink, luxuries, marriage — but enjoy it *now*. This meaningless life which God gives you will soon be over. Put away anything mournful or serious and live life to the full. Soon you will not be able to. You are going to the grave, where there is no activity, no planning and no wisdom (7-10).

c. Because life is uncertain (9:11-16)
In this life there is no telling who will win or lose. People do not always receive what we would expect, or what they deserve. We are all victims of time and chance (11). Then, when death comes, it always does so unexpectedly (12). Credit does not always (or even usually) come to those who deserve it — as Solomon's illustration of a poor man, who saved a besieged city by his wisdom, so eloquently

shows (13-16).

Although this time the point is only made implicitly, the purpose of this paragraph is the same as that of the previous two. Because life is unpredictable, and no one knows when it will end, the thing to do is to live for the *here and now.* Human logic, unenlightened by God's revelation, must inevitably come to this conclusion. As it was three thousand years ago, when Solomon wrote, so it is today.

2. 9:17 - 10:20. Lessons worth learning

None the less, unconverted men and women are still able to make helpful observations about life. We have proved this a thousand times — for instance, in the helpful books and magazines which we have read, the vast majority of which were written by unconverted people. Human reason is certainly affected by sin, as is every other aspect of human life and personality, but this does not mean that every conclusion which an unregenerate person reaches is invalid. They are still able to notice that some lives are better than others. If this were not so, Solomon's previous sermon could never have made its point. Although written from an earth-bound perspective, the section which follows is very similar to the second half of the third sermon. It is a catalogue of valid observations made by an unconverted man. They are so wise that we might be forgiven if we began thinking that we were reading the book of Proverbs!

a. About wisdom and folly (9:17 - 10:15)

Earth-bound Solomon, advising us to live for the here and now, cannot help noticing that those who are rushing so fast to the grave do not all live lives of the same quality. Nor do they all speak the same. There is such a thing as a wise use of words (9:17-18; 10:12-14).

In 9:17-18 Solomon seems to be suggesting that what he has just written in 9:16 is not always true. Wisdom is *not* always despised. It does not *always* go unheeded. The quiet speech of a wise man is listened to much more readily than the clamorous chatterings of someone who simply loves the sound of his own voice. Wisdom accomplishes more than weapons do, despite the fact that one sinner can ruin its good effects. The service of the wise man remains worthwhile after all. What a contrast there is between the speech of a wise man, and that of a fool! (10:12-14) One is gracious and winsome, the other talks excessively, and his words are foolish from beginning to end. He gives the impression that he knows what the future holds — but who does?

Wisdom and folly can be contrasted in the realm of conduct, as well as in that of words. This is seen in 10:2-4, 8-11. A wise man goes to his work with application, with dexterity; but a fool with awkwardness (2). Indeed, the fool advertises his folly wherever he goes (3), whereas the wise person knows how foolish hasty action is, and what is to be gained by retaining one's composure (4). It is the use of the mind which is the major difference between the wise and the foolish. The wise man always thinks of the dangers, and proceeds with prudence. He considers how best his task may be done, and prepares properly for it (8-10). Knowing *when* to exercise your skill is also all-important, as the wise man knows. If you know how to charm a snake, but do not do so before it bites you, what have you gained? (11)

What a difference there is between wisdom and folly! (10:1, 5-7, 15) Just as the odour from the decaying body of a fly can ruin the expensive perfume in which it became entrapped, so the tiniest folly can undo all the benefits of a large amount of wisdom (1). Many people have become prominent in public life on the strength of their good judgement. Who can tell how many of them have later been ruined or disgraced as the result of a single indiscretion? And what an awful thing it is when folly is elevated to a position that only wisdom should occupy! (5-7) The chief

thing about a fool is that he talks a lot (14a), but he will
actually labour to the point of exhaustion without accom-
plishing anything. He just cannot see the obvious way to
reach the goal, although it is as plain as plain can be (15).

b. *About the rule of kings (10:16-20)*
From wisdom and folly Solomon passes to a related subject
— principles of government. How dreadful it is when authority is in the hands of an inexperienced ruler, aided by
unscrupulous advisers, who are idle when they should be
working! (16) But when government is in the hand of the
experienced, who have no interest in self-indulgence, but
whose every activity is harnessed to help them in their task
— how blessed is the land! (17)

Laziness is a great evil. It accomplishes nothing, but is
certain to cause things to end in ruin (18). Feasts are made
for laughter, and wine is bought so that people can make
merry. But neither can be enjoyed without money (19).
Solomon evidently still has in his mind the foolish rulers
who have lives of luxurious idleness and squander the
money entrusted to them. It is an abuse which unregenerate
men and women still feel strongly about.

None the less, Solomon counsels us to be careful about
criticizing rulers, even in the privacy of our bedrooms, and
even in our thoughts. It is likely that we shall be summoned
before the ruler we have criticized, who will inform us
that 'a little birdie' has told him of our opinions! (20)

At this point Solomon closes the first part of this final
sermon, with its vivid account of how unconverted man
thinks. In some areas those who live without God are
exceedingly wise. But not when it comes to weighing up
the meaning of life. At this point they are at a loss as
to what to say. Their whole view is this-worldly and
materialistic. Their philosophy is ultimately one of
despair. Knowing that death will soon rob them of everything they have ever lived for, they wonder what the point

of it all is. Life is unsatisfying and meaningless. There is only one thing to do — to live for the moment, for the here and now.

II – Purpose (11:1 - 12:7)

1. *11:1-8. Do good whenever you can*

Solomon's writing from a godly perspective begins with a proverb which is exceedingly well known, but which is notoriously difficult to explain (1). It is a case where the illustration is not clear, although the lesson is. The converted person's view is that he should not live for himself. This is the exact opposite of the overall view of the unconverted, which we have just studied. Instead of indulging ourselves with what we have earned, we should be generous in giving it away, even if it appears for the moment that such generosity is entirely wasted. It is not. Our gifts will eventually come back to us, and we shall at last profit by our action.

We should give generously, because we may not always have the opportunity to do so (2). The usefulness of the clouds lies in the fact that they empty themselves (3a).

We should let nothing discourage us from this duty. When a tree falls it is no use thinking, 'It might have been better if it had fallen in a different direction.' The simple fact is that it did not, and we have got to face the situation as it is. We must not spend our days pondering 'might have beens' (3b). Nor must we wait for ideal conditions before we start doing what is right. If we wait for everything to be 'just right' we will never get *anything* done! (4) What potent lessons there are to learn here, for every area of life — but especially for those involved in Christian work!

There are lots of things which we do not know in this life (5). But there is one thing we *do* know — that there is

no reaping without sowing. So get on with it! *Be* generous!
Do good! There will be nothing accomplished unless you
do (6). The time to work is *now*. We must work while we
can, because the time is coming when we will not be able
to (7-8).

2. *11:9 - 12:7. Serve God while you are young*
If you are young, go on, enjoy your youth and vitality.
Satisfy your heart's desires in intelligent pleasure. Be as
carefree as you can. But remember that youth does not
last, and that God will judge you for the way you have
used these years (9-10).

Now is the time to remember God, while life is a thing
to enjoy and not to endure, and before the declining years
set in (1). All too soon a storm will overcloud the present
noonday of your life. The days of warmth, brightness and
unrestrained enjoyment will then be over (2). Hands and
arms will begin to tremble, legs to bend with weakness;
teeth will be few and eyes dim (3). Your ears will no longer
hear, and your teeth will cease to grind. Unable to sleep,
you will rise at the crack of dawn; and you will have less
voice, particularly for singing (4).

The days are coming when you will dread walking up
hills, and will actually be afraid of going out. A grey-haired
old person, you will be so weak that you will hardly be
able to drag yourself along (5). The remainder of this verse
refers to failing sexual desire. The craver berry, referred to
here, was an aphrodisiac which stimulated sexual appetite.
At last you will go to your eternal home, and the mourners
will be heard in the streets (5b).

Soon the silver chain fastening it to the ceiling will
break, and the golden oil-lamp will come crashing to the
floor. The oil will spill out from the broken bowl and your
light will be extinguished. To change the picture of death,
the pitcher will be shattered and unable to carry any more
of the water of life. The wheel at the well will be broken

and no more water will be brought up from it (6). At last you will die. Death is the separation of body and spirit. The body will return to the ground from which it was made, and the spirit to God who gave it, and in whose hands is its eternal destiny (7). All these things are certainties. So serve God now — while you can; and while you are still in full enjoyment of your faculties (1).

Unconverted people, as we have seen, think in terms of living for themselves. The certain approach of death makes them decide to enjoy themselves while they can. They reason that every other thought should be put aside, and that we should concentrate on indulging ourselves here and now. Who knows what the future holds? Therefore live for the present!

Solomon's counsel from the divine standpoint is a complete contradiction of such thinking. While life can be enjoyed, he advises, turn to God, without whom life has no purpose. While you have your faculties, use them — but never forgetting him while you do so.

How often the excitement of being young causes young people to forget God! They think that they have plenty of time to consider him *later*. He is all right for old people, but an irrelevance for youth. Yet when old age comes their character has become too set in its ways to launch itself into holy thoughts. In very many elderly people all desire for spiritual things has been poisoned by bitterness. Tired bodies and senile minds frequently render them quite incapable of even consciously registering what they hear about God. They find that old age is *too late* to turn to him!

How few there are who come to the Lord in later years! To magnify his grace God saves some at this stage in life, but hardly any. This should not surprise us when we have read such as a passage as the one we have just considered. There is a favoured time to seek and find the Lord. There is a favoured time to serve him. That time is *youth*!

7.
Epilogue   (12:8-14)

Please read Ecclesiastes 12:8-14

Almost the whole of the book of Ecclesiastes is now behind us. The opening verses introduced us to Solomon looking at life through the eyes of an unconverted man. Through the four sermons which followed we saw him alternate between that viewpoint and that of a man in fellowship with God. Only the few verses of the epilogue now remain. Will they contain anything new?

1. *12:8. The conclusion of the earth-bound man*
There is nothing new about the opening verse of the epilogue. Throughout the book we have heard the unconverted person's cry of 'Futility!' and we hear it here for the final time. From an unregenerate point of view there is nothing more to say. Life *is* meaningless. Whatever lessons may have been learned, however wise have been one's observations, thoughts, words and deeds — all comes to nothing. The grave awaits us, and who knows if there is anything beyond it? A man without God can ultimately do nothing more than wring his hands and join his voice to that of the Preacher's: 'Futility of futility . . . *all* is futility.'

2. *12:9-12. The aim and authority of the Preacher*
But Solomon is not content to sign off on that note. Before he pens his closing words, he wants to tell us why he wrote his book. His aim throughout was to communicate wisdom to others. He did not do this haphazardly, but made every effort to select his material carefully, to set it out in order,

and to put it across in a memorable way (9). By deliberately choosing pleasing words he did his best to make it interesting, so as to gain and keep the attention of his hearers and readers. But he did not do this at the expense of truth. This was something he was never willing to sacrifice (10).

Such words, he tells us, are goads, to prod and spur us into action. They are nails, to which we can securely affix our lives. The nails may well be fastened by a multitude of wise instructors, but they are all derived from *one* Shepherd (11). Solomon is obviously claiming nothing less than divine inspiration for what he has written.

This being so, he affectionately counsels us to give attention to his words. There is no need to give ourselves to a never-ending and wearying search for the meaning of life. Verse 12 is not intended to discourage us from all study, but is a warning against useless and tiring reading and studying which seeks to unravel life's mystery. There is no need for it. The answer for which we are searching is *here,* in this divinely inspired, humanly transmitted book of Ecclesiastes.

The whole book contains the answer, but Solomon's closing words are a summary of his preceding pages. He is anxious that everyone should grasp the message, and that nobody should misunderstand.

3. *12:13-14. The conclusion of the matter*
For this reason the teaching of the entire book is now gathered up into two weighty sentences, so phrased that they can be remembered easily. No one need ever mistake what conclusion the book has come to. Instructions for living the only life worth living can be encapsulated in a few straightforward words which can be recalled effortlessly in every situation which we face.

In Hebrew the last phrase of verse 13 reads, 'This is every man.' In other words, 'This is every man's duty.' Whoever we are, whatever may be our nationality or circumstances, and in whatever period of history we have lived, two things are required of us. These are what we should live for. It was for these that we were made, and without them we can secure neither fulfilment nor happiness.

The first is the fear of God. This does not mean being *terrified* of him. The Bible never uses this expression in that way. It does not have in mind a guilty cringing before him. It means, rather, having a reverent respect for him, because of his greatness and glory. To this is added gratitude for his kindness and mercy, awe at his power, confidence in his wisdom, submission to his will and delight in the experience of communing with him. Besides all this, the person who fears God has a deep affection for him, such as a child might have for a parent.

The fear of God is a habit of mind which acknowledges him at every step, and which views everything in relation to him who is eternally holy, just and good. It is not the degrading and demoralizing dread of his power such as can be found in many pagan religions, but an inward attitude which loves him, is aware that life is lived in his presence and which longs to please him. It nurses the sincere and heartfelt intention to live life, not for oneself, but *for him!* Ecclesiastes insists that the only life worth living is the one which has such a fear as this as its motivation and mainspring.

The second duty is not separate from the first, but arises from it. The inward life of a man or woman shows itself outwardly. Those whose hearts are set on pleasing God just cannot be the same as others. The homage of their heart is carried over into their life, and they discipline themselves to live in open and unashamed obedience to God's commands. They are not interested in a mere external compliance. They are no fans of the Pharisees. Their outward actions are the manifestation of their spiritual loyalty and love. They submit their wills to the authority of their heavenly Lord, and put aside all feelings and emotions which endanger their obedience. They are out *to honour God.* They do his will cheerfully, never flagging in their efforts to cultivate a God-fearing spirit and a blameless life.

This is the life worth living, but if we should ever doubt it (as we inevitably do, from time to time), there is something we should remember. This present life is not the whole of existence. Death is not the end. There is to come a future judgement at which the godly will openly receive God's favour, and the ungodly the due punishment they deserve. God himself will be the Judge, and he will hold us personally accountable for the way that we have lived. We shall answer directly to him as to whether or not we have attended to the duty which he has laid upon us. There is to be a final proof that the only life worth living is the one lived *for him.*

We make a big mistake if we think that the consequences which our particular life deserves are reaped in this world. That is a myth. We have seen it exploded several times in this book. It is a future judgement that we have to attend, where every detail of our lives will be surveyed by the eye of an omniscient and unerring God. How awful to fare badly then! How wonderful to fare well!

Then our characters will be seen as they really are. 'God shall bring every work into judgement, with every secret thing' (14). The Syriac ends, '. . . and manifest thing', and the Septuagint, '. . . with everything that has been overlooked'. But the point has been well made without these additions. The scrutiny of God extends to the secret part of our lives, to the evil as well as the good. Hidden things will be exposed and undiscovered crimes revealed. All we consider private will be public at last. In God's assessment of our lives nothing will be omitted or forgotten. We shall stand before a Judge who is absolutely just, wise, free from all partiality, and whose sentence is final. This truth is nowhere else so forcibly stated in the Old Testament and is, of course, repeated with renewed emphasis in the New.

This is the great fact to be called to mind when it is questioned whether godly living is worthwhile. The truth of a future judgement is known to every person's conscience (Romans 1:32), but its details are stated clearly in God's revelation. It is this revelation which has enlightened our minds. There is no other evidence of such a judgement, but we know that it is true, none the less. We have learned not to judge by appearances. We live in a world where wicked people sometimes get credit for goodness which does not belong to them, and where the good are often maligned and misunderstood. But all will be put straight in the future, when every individual will be judged, not according to what he appears to be, but according to what he really is.

What will then happen to those who have lived and died without so much as a thought for God? It is unthinkable that they will possibly meet with his favour when they stand before him. The supreme folly of living as they have done will at last be revealed. All that they have ever lived for will have come to nothing. A life filled with a sense of futility will be followed by eternal disaster.

That sense of futility is absent from the believer. He knows what the purpose of life is, and what must follow. He sees that lasting happiness lies in the simple but profound recognition that 'Man's chief end is to glorify God, and to enjoy him for ever'.

On this Solomon's book has been clear. The purpose for which it was written has been fulfilled. Yet it has left us, like Thomas, with an unanswered question. The *way* to God has not been made plain. 'How *can* we know the way?' (John 14:5.)

'Jesus saith unto him, I am the way, the truth, and the life: no man cometh unto the Father, but by me' (John 14:6).

How grateful we are that there is more to the Bible than Ecclesiastes! Solomon has shown us that by nature we inhabit the city of futility and destruction. We would be better off if we lived in the city of communion with God. But it is only in the gospel of our Lord Jesus Christ that the way there is made plain.

A Lord worth loving:
Song of Solomon

8.
Some things to say first

Next to Ecclesiastes, in our English Bibles, we find the
Song of Solomon. The arrangement of the Hebrew Bible is
different, and yet there, too, both books are in close prox-
imity, being found in the *megilloth* or 'five rolls'. To keep
a balance in our spiritual lives it is important that we
should not study one of these books without the other.
Ecclesiastes focuses on our intellect, our mental outlook.
The Song of Solomon focuses on our emotions, and
especially on the emotion of love. Ecclesiastes tells us that
life is not worth living unless we live it for God. The Song
of Solomon teaches us that living for the Lord means
loving him. The two books together reveal that both head
and heart must be given over to God.

Background

This book, wrote an ancient rabbi, is 'a gift of inestimable
value to Israel, and the holiest of all sacred writings'. The
Jews revered it as uniquely sublime, and sang portions of it
on each day of their first and greatest national festival, the
eight days of Passover and unleavened bread. To them
Proverbs was like the outer court of the temple, Ecclesiastes
like the holy place, but the Song of Solomon as the holy
of holies.

'Holy of holies' is an expression familiar to most of us,
and means 'the holiest place of all'. Such repetition was a
common Hebrew way of expressing superlatives. 'King of
kings and Lord of lords' means that, of all kings and lords,
Christ is the highest and most important. In the same way,

73

this book announces itself as 'The song of songs' (1:1). Many songs came from Solomon's pen (1 Kings 4:32), but none of the others could be put in the same class as this one. This was nobler and more wonderful than them all. The Song is very often also called 'Canticles' (series of songs), because in fact thirteen songs make up the one song of the book.

The first verse can be translated, 'The song of songs which is *about* or *concerning* Solomon,' but this need not cause us to deviate from the historic view that he was the author of the book. His name appears at 1:1,5; 3:7,9,11; 8:11-12. The excellence of the book is certainly fully in harmony with the great wisdom which we know he possessed (1 Kings 4:32-33). But we cannot tell precisely when he wrote the book. It was obviously before his apostasy recorded in 1 Kings 11:3-4, and yet the unusually large number of foreign words in the text show that it was after he had sustained and widespread contact with surrounding nations. We have, then, in our hands a poem written roughly around 965 B.C.

The Song of Solomon is like a chain of thirteen links, all of different sizes. It can be looked upon as a single poem, or as thirteen poems of varying lengths linked together. This does not suggest that there is anything disjointed about it. A similar refrain occurs several times (at 2:7; 3:5, 8:4), the same characters appear again and again, and the vivid imagery is the same throughout the book. Some of the poetic figures of speech seem most unusual to those of us who do not live in the Middle East. At no point in our study must we lose sight of the fact that we are reading an oriental love poem.

The setting of the story

The story of Solomon's poem centres on a single pair, but

the various canticles are linked together by the appearance and reappearance of subordinate groups, such as the 'daughters of Jerusalem' (1:5; 2:7; 3:10; 5:8,16) and the 'watchmen' (3:3; 5:7), and also by the recurrence of significant refrains (see 2:17; 4:6; 2:16; 6:3; 7:10).

The pair is composed of Solomon, who is the chief character, and a Shulamite woman. The expression 'Shulamite' is found only at 6:13, and probably means that she was a native of Shunem, a village near the plain of Megiddo, a little north of Jezreel. Some people believe that the story also has a third main character — a shepherd lover, to whom the Shulamite remains loyal despite the advances of Solomon. A plausible case can be made for this suggestion, but I, for one, have never found it totally convincing. H.A. Ironside's summary of the story[1] seems much more reasonable. It can be put in the following way.

King Solomon had a vineyard in the hill country of Ephraim, about fifty miles north of Jerusalem, which he let out to keepers (8:11). These keepers consisted of a mother, her two sons and their younger sister, the Shulamite (1:6; 6:13; 8:8). The Shulamite was the 'Cinderella' of the family, naturally beautiful, but unnoticed (1:5). Very probably her brothers were half-brothers (1:6). They made her work very hard in the vineyard, so that she had virtually no time to care for her personal appearance (1:6). She pruned the vines, set the traps for the little foxes, kept the flocks, and was out in the open so much that she became extremely sunburned (2:15; 1:8,5).

One day, disguised, Solomon arrived at the vineyard and showed an interest in her (1:6). She took him to be a shepherd and asked him about his flocks (1:7). He answered evasively, but also spoke loving words to her and promised

1. See H.A. Ironside, *Addresses on The Song of Solomon*, pp. 17-21, usefully summarized by Merrill Unger in *Unger's Bible Handbook*, pp. 299-300.

her rich gifts in the future (1:8-11). He won her heart and left with the promise that he would return some day. That night she dreamed of him, and sometimes thought that he was near (3:1). Finally he *did* return, in all his kingly splendour, and took her to be his bride (3:6-7).

Schools of interpretation

But how is this beautiful poem, containing this story, to be interpreted? Through the centuries there have been basically three different approaches.

1. *Allegorical*
This school of thought sees the Song as entirely figurative. It has no foundation in historical fact. The events which it records never actually took place, but are simply pictures of something else.

This has always been the most common interpretation among the Jews. For them the Song expressed the relationship of love which exists between Jehovah and his chosen people. It was only on this basis that they saw fit to admit the book into their canon of Scripture. How else could they have received a book which has as its theme love between humans, contains only one reference to God (see 8:6 in a modern version), never mentions sin or any religious theme, does not quote any other part of Scripture and is never quoted itself?

An allegorical interpretation has also been dominant in the Christian church since the time of Origen (about A.D. 185-254). Christians have noted that the book is not quoted by the Lord Jesus Christ or by the New Testament Scriptures, though there is an allusion to 4:7 in Ephesians 5:27. For them the allegory speaks of the love which binds together Christ and his church.

Modern versions of the allegorical interpretation have

laid some emphasis on the supposed third character of the story — the shepherd lover referred to earlier. He is seen as a type of Christ, the Shulamite as a type of the Christian believer, and Solomon as a type of this sinful world, trying to woo the believer away from his first love. If this *is* so, it presents us with an insuperable problem. We have Solomon writing about himself and typifying himself as a figure of the worst sort of temptation that a believer has to face. It hardly seems likely, does it?

But the older allegorical interpretations face difficulties, too. They ignore the fact that the book contains fifteen or more identifiable geographical references, and that it therefore does have a certain factual basis. But, even worse, they tie themselves in knots trying to find a spiritual meaning for every single allusion and turn of phrase which the book contains. The task is impossible, and those who attempt it have to resort to boundless ingenuity and inventiveness, rather than to solid principles of biblical interpretation. Are we really to believe that every plant and herb mentioned in Canticles has a distinct and important spiritual significance?

2. *Naturalistic*

The naturalistic school of interpretation sees the Song as a poem extolling human love, carrying no typical or figurative meaning whatever. Its intention is to show that physical beauty and married love are good and perfect in their place, and that we should not despise them. Only in marriage is human love, in all its aspects, truly fulfilled. The book teaches us how to love, to admire God's creation of the human body and, in particular, to see our own faults in married love.

This view finds support in the fact that aspects of physical love are frankly mentioned throughout the Song, but always in a pure and lofty manner. They are never considered as something lewd or licentious. But there is a problem. Our Lord Jesus Christ assures us that he is to be found in all the Old Testament Scriptures. He is their subject and theme (Luke 24:27, 44-48). But according to the naturalistic interpretation, he is not in this book at all! If this school of thought is right, our Lord was wrong!

3. *Typical*

The typical school of interpretation sees the characters and events of the Song of Solomon as suggestive of spiritual truths, without there being an exact equivalence, as in an allegory. This view is best summed up in the following words of Dr G. Campbell Morgan: 'The songs should be treated then, first as simple and yet sublime songs of human affection. When they are thus understood, reverently the thoughts may be lifted into the higher value of setting forth the joys of the communion between the spirit of man and the Spirit of God, and ultimately between the Church and Christ.'[2]

This seems to be the only tenable view. It escapes the difficulties of the two other views in that it honours the book's factual basis, does not need to resort to fancies of imagination to see a spiritual meaning in every word, and yet sees Christ in the Song. Although justice may be done to the actual language of this oriental love poem, the bride is a *type* of the church, and Solomon of the Lord Jesus Christ. In thinking of their mutual love we cannot escape thinking of a love which is higher and better. Our study of the poem enriches our understanding of the Lord's love towards us and instructs us concerning what love we should show in return.

Under this view we have no difficulty in joining with the naturalistic school and seeing the Song as a book intended to honour pure human love and the marriage bond. We note

2. G. Campbell Morgan, *The Analyzed Bible*, (Westwood, N.J: Revell, 1964) p.197.

that its frank and intimate expressions of love often prove embarrassing to some readers, and begin to understand why no ancient Jew was ever allowed to read the Song before his thirtieth birthday. Yet Solomon's poem succeeds in showing us that physical attraction and love can be enjoyed without sensual lust and uncleanness. Our reaction to the world's degraded abuse of physical love is not to be an ascetic abstinence but, rather, pure enjoyment.

But we cannot agree with the naturalistic school that this is as far as the book goes. We simply cannot help seeing Christ here. The theme of love causes regenerate minds to turn naturally to thinking of him. Every mention of love causes us to meditate on *his* and to bemoan the poverty of our own response. We think of our union with him and long for a closer communion. We find ourselves overwhelmed at his tenderness towards us and the sheer bliss of belonging to him for ever. Our own love towards him is at last excited a little. We feel that we cannot live without him and desire him as never before. We know that we can never close our hearts to him again, and many expressions of the book become the language of our own devotion. Our typical approach ceases to be an academic approach and our reading of the book becomes a precious spiritual experience. We desire nothing less for every reader.

Structure

At first sight the structure of the Song of Solomon seems rather confusing, but closer examination shows that the book has three main sections.

1:1 - 3:5 deal with the courtship days of Solomon and the Shulamite. The chief speaker in this section is the Shulamite who, as a bride, muses over the events which led up to her wedding.

3:6 - 5:1 are about the wedding itself. We are given the

privilege of being onlookers as the bridal procession passes
on its way to Jerusalem, and of being guests at the wedding
feast. In this section the main speaker is the bridegroom,
and we listen in to a traditional speech in praise of the
bride, which is still an important part of many Eastern
weddings.

5:2 - 8:14 tell us about the married life of the happy
pair, and this section breaks down into three smaller units.
5:2 - 6:3 reveal that, shortly after her marriage, the Shulamite dreamed of an experience that alienated her from
Solomon. The passage describes the agony she went through
until there was a reunion. 6:4 - 8:4 find Solomon as the
main speaker again, and we learn how the restored love
relationship between the couple grew stronger with time
and experience. The short closing paragraph of 8:5-14 wit-
nesses both husband and wife speaking equally, and the
theme is that of their settled devotion to each other.

In this way the book has a natural progression. We see
love awakened and its first attempts to express itself. We
see the lovers coming into union with each other. Their
love is then tried and tested, but emerges as mature, settled
and triumphant. It is at this climax that the book closes.

A necessary warning

Once we spot this natural progression, the Song of Solomon
becomes really quite easy to follow. Until then it appears
to be 'bitty' and incoherent. It does not seem to be going
anywhere. But from the moment we detect that it moves
from courtship to marriage, and then at last to the experience of mutual love, it begins to make sense.

But the very recognition of this progression can lead us
into new dangers. In contradiction of the typical approach
which we have adopted, we may find ourselves uncon-
sciously allegorizing the poem. Perhaps we begin to think

of the courtship passage as the believer's experience of
Christ before conversion, of the wedding as conversion
itself and of the remainder of the poem as what follows
conversion.

If we start to do that sort of thing we shall find ourselves
in trouble. Can our pre-conversion days honestly be
described in the terms set forth in 1:1 - 3:5? If the wedding
of chapter 4 equals conversion, why does the New Testament speak of the marriage supper of the Lamb as a *future*
event? Shall we then alter our view, and interpret chapter 4
as referring to that glorious event? If we do, what are we
to make of the troubled dream of separation which *follows*
it? Can the believer be separated from Christ *after* the
second coming? Surely, that is impossible!

And this is not the only trouble we get into. If we are
not married to Christ until the end of the world, where
does 2 Corinthians 11:2 fit in? If the wedding is still a
future event, how can Paul in Ephesians 5 be referring to
this in relation to the *present* duties of husbands and wives?

Any allegorizing of the Song of Solomon is certain to
tie us up in knots. If we cannot do it as far as the broad
sections of the poem are concerned, how much less can we
do it when we come to its details! The whole point of the
typical interpretation is that it insists that there is *no exact
equivalence* between any movement or detail of the poem
and the relationship which exists between Christ and his
people. One is suggestive of the other, no doubt. But it is
quite impossible to put down the poem and the New
Testament's teaching in parallel columns, and to show how
one is the exact pictorial equivalent of the other.

Why bother, then, to show that the Song has these
distinct movements? And why bother to spend so many of
the following pages simply explaining the meaning of the
poem's details?

The answer is easy. It is only as we are enjoying this
oriental love poem *in its own right* that our minds will rise

naturally to ponder a higher and better love. But how are we ever to enjoy it, if we simply do not understand it?

The spiritual person's thoughts will rise spontaneously from the Song to the Lord Jesus Christ, *provided that he knows what the Song is saying*. It is this that this short commentary seeks to make clear. It was the only reason for writing it. This introduction has served part of that purpose, but we can now get no further unless we take down our Bibles and study the Song for ourselves . . .

9.
Courtship days   (1:1-3:5)

The Shulamite	Solomon
1:2-7	
	1:8-11
1:12-14	
	1:15
1:16-17	
	2:1-2
2:3-9	
	2:10-15
2:16 - 3:5	

9.
Courtship days (1:1-3:5)

Please read the Song of Solomon 1:1 - 3:5

Although the bridegroom also speaks and the 'daughters of Jerusalem' are alluded to, the main speaker in this first section is the Shulamite, who appears as a bride reflecting on her courtship days with Solomon. Throughout our studies we shall simply look at the book as it stands, but we will expect our thoughts to rise constantly to that higher relationship of love which binds the Lord Jesus Christ to those who belong to him.

1:2-7. The Shulamite
She recalls the attractiveness of her beloved, and her own lack of it
2.　As the book opens, the bride expresses her great love and longing for her lover. Today we often associate kissing with loose infatuation or sensual desire. In the Bible it is an expression of pure and deep love, though it has several other meanings, too: an expression of affection, a pledge of peace, a token of reconciliation and a sign of acceptance.

The Bible frequently associates wine with joy and gladness. But better than wine, which gladdens the heart, is the love of the bridegroom for the bride — the greatest delight she knows.
3.　On account of the heat, ointments and perfumes are used widely in the East. It is necessary to wash several times a day, and afterwards the skin is treated with sweet-smelling oils. Not unnaturally, royal people had ointments of rare composition and unusual fragrance. It is such a fragrance

84

that the Shulamite has in mind as she contemplates her
lover. His name — in other words, all that he is — is fragrant.
She has boundless admiration for him, and cannot but
think that others will be filled with affection for him,
too.

4.   In verse 2 the bride expressed how much she wanted
the bridegroom to come to her. Now she expresses the
desire that she may be drawn after him. In her musing she
sees herself as in his immediate presence. What joy! She
wishes to share this joy with others. It is no mistake for
them to have such an affection for him. It is fully justified.

5.   Up to this point her language has all been about Solomon's attractiveness. Her natural beauty had been spoiled
by the sun, which had burned her as black as the tents of
Kedar — a nomadic tribe descended from Kedar, whose
tents were made from black or dark brown goatskin. But
although her beauty was spoiled, it was still there. The
Shulamite is thus able to compare herself with the attractive and multicoloured curtains found in Solomon's palace.

6.   H.A. Ironside postulates that the opening words of
this verse are the actual words which the Shulamite spoke
to Solomon when she first met him. In her reminiscing she
recalls them exactly. But the fault was not hers. For a
reason not mentioned, her half-brothers had become
incensed with her, and had put her to keep the vineyard.
They had treated her so harshly that she had been unable
to give any time to caring for her personal complexion.
Yet it was to this unattractive person that the all-lovely
king had come, and to whom he had given his royal love!

7.   She recalls just how much she had longed to be with
him then. He had come in the guise of a shepherd, but she
had felt that she could not wait until evening to see him
and had hoped that she could find him during the noonday
rest. Why should she be as others — or as ignorant of his
whereabouts as someone blindfolded — when she could be
with him?

1:8-11.   Solomon
He says how he admires her and promises gifts

8.   If she does not know the way to him, he tells her, this is all she has to do. She will discover him as she walks the path of duty. It is in fulfilling her responsibilities as a shepherdess that she will be certain to meet him. The following of duty is the way to delight. Who can miss the spiritual lesson of such a verse as this?

9.   The bridegroom now reveals his opinion of the bride. He finds her strikingly beautiful, graceful and with admirable traits of character. There are probably not many ladies reading this who would appreciate being compared to a horse, let alone a company of them! But in the East, where the beauty of horses is particularly valued, this would be an outstandingly high compliment.

10-11.   Perhaps he is still thinking of horses when he says how her ornaments accentuate the beauty of her cheeks and neck. In any event, he promises her new ornaments to enhance her beauty even further. It is a wonder that the king should ever love the unlovely. But what shall be said about the fact that he also beautifies her? W.J. Cameron comments at this point, 'However much grace the Church may have received and may exhibit, Christ has more to bestow, to make her more acceptable to Himself.'

1:12-14.   The Shulamite
She expresses her satisfaction with her beloved

12.   Spikenard is a plant of Indian origin, from which was extracted an extremely precious and highly valued aromatic oil (see Mark 14:3-5). The sweet smell of this nard, imported into Palestine from the earliest times, is seen by the Shulamite as an appropriate symbol of her love for Solomon.

13.   Myrrh is also a fragrant substance prepared from plants, and was imported from both India and Arabia. The ancient world considered it to be useful as a disinfectant,

and also believed that it had reviving qualities. For this reason it was often put into small bags or pendants and worn, night and day, around the neck or between the breasts. The Shulamite cannot envisage being without her beloved, whom she regards as being unspeakably precious and fragrant.

14.   Camphire or henna is a small shrub found particularly in the valley of Engedi, an oasis on the western shore of the Dead Sea. It carries clusters of white and yellow flowers, which have an unusual fragrance. It is naturally highly valued, and this is the point of the allusion here. How highly the Shulamite thought of Solomon!

1:15.   Solomon
He praises the loveliness of the Shulamite
15.   Biblically the dove is often a symbol of innocence. However, as the passage is about physical beauty, Solomon is almost certainly referring to something physical, rather than to the qualities of purity, grace, constancy and tenderness to which some writers refer. He is struck by the sparkling beauty of her eyes. To him, there is nobody like her.

1:16-17.   The Shulamite
She expresses her pleasure in her beloved and in her surroundings
16-17.   Here the bride replies to Solomon, using of him terms which are very similar to those he used of her. What follows is a description of imaginary surroundings, where she thinks of herself as being with him. We need not think that the Shulamite is thinking of an actual place in the woodland, or of a booth erected on the flat roof of a house. It is an attempt to express how she feels about their great love for each other. We do the same sort of thing ourselves. For instance our hymns, when speaking of the future bliss of being with Christ in heaven, talk of 'green pastures'

and 'bright skies'. It is a mistake to take such poetic terms literally.

2:1-2.   Solomon
He compares himself and the Shulamite to flowers,
suggestive of beauty and grace
1.   Sharon lay to the south of Carmel, on the Mediterranean coast, and was a place of great fertility. There grew many brightly coloured flowers, or 'lilies' as the Arabs call any such plant. The 'rose of Sharon' is probably the sweet-scented narcissus, which is greatly prized in the East, though there are some who think that the reference is to the crimson anemone. Whichever way it is, the meaning of the verse is clear. The bridegroom presents himself as an object of admiration and delight.
2.   Conscious of his own attractiveness, the bridegroom now speaks of hers. So far as lilies surpass thistles, so does she surpass others. It is quite common for the anemone to be surrounded by thorns, and the contrast serves to emphasize its beauty. In a similar way, the Shulamite is outstanding to Solomon.

2:3-9.   The Shulamite
She tells of her delight in the fellowship of her beloved
3.   The bride replies in the same vein. As an apple tree, with its delicious fruit and restful shade, is so much better than other trees, so her beloved stands apart from others. To her there is simply nobody like him, and he is a person that she *enjoys.*
4.   She now uses another picture to speak of her enjoyment of his love. Although she is a country girl of no status, he has brought her into his palace. As a bride, surrounded by the feasting of her wedding day, and covered by the panoply which is a feature of Jewish weddings, she wonders at the love which has made her so privileged.
5-6.   She is so overcome with love and admiration for her

lover, that she has to ask for raisin cakes and apples to
sustain her physically. A similar experience is not unknown
to those who walk closely with Christ. W.J. Cameron
recounts how the Covenanter John Welch was so filled
with 'the sensible enjoyment of God' during his last illness,
that he was sometimes heard to pray, 'Lord, hold thine
hand; it is enough; thy servant is but a clay vessel and can
hold no more.' This was the effect on the Shulamite as her
beloved embraced her.

7.   At this point the Shulamite gives the first of her recur-
ring charges to the oft-appearing 'daughters of Jerusalem'.
Apparently no real oath is intended, as it is given in the
name of animals. Why roes or gazelles are chosen, we do
not know. But the meaning of the adjuration is plain. They
are not to awaken her love prematurely. Love is a very
tender commodity, and easily harmed. It must awaken
itself, and at its own speed, and must not be fanned up by
others.

8-9.   Verse 8 begins a new canticle, but it is still the
Shulamite talking. In verses 8-17 we surely have some of
the most beautiful poetry ever written. Is the bride still
reminiscing? Is she recalling the time when she had not
seen Solomon for the whole of the winter? But now spring
has broken she sees him coming, leaping with ease and
grace like a gazelle. Now he is by the wall, and now appear-
ing at the lattice. She cannot see him perfectly, but she
does have some sight of him. And she is thrilled!

2:10-15.   Solomon
His invitation

10-13.   He calls her to go with him. In *The Wycliffe Bible
Commentary* Sierd Woudstra comments, 'Here . . . the
imagery of the seasons is introduced. The latter suggests
that bride and bridegroom have reached the proper state of
maturity for the fruition of their mutual love.' If this is so,
it is in direct contrast to verse 7.

14.   He continues his call by using a term of close endearment, 'my dove'. The reference is to the rock pigeon, which chooses to hide itself in the clefts of high cliffs or deep ravines. He is beseeching her to come out, so that he can see her face again and hear her voice.

15.   Their love is about to burst into full fruition. Nothing, however small, must be allowed to prevent this, or to hinder its full enjoyment.

2:16-17. The Shulamite
Her declaration and desire

16.   This verse should be compared with 6:3 and 7:10. The Shulamite is confident that she and her bridegroom belong to each other. She pictures him as a shepherd who, during the daytime, is away from her, but who is fulfilling his task in the most beautiful of places — a place totally in keeping with his own beauty and honour.

17.   They belong to each other, she knows, for ever. The imagery is of the heat of the day giving way to the cool of evening, when the shadows cast by the sun are disappearing. When that time comes she expects her beloved to cross the mountains that now separate them, and for there to be a joyful reunion. The whole verse conveys the yearning desire that the couple have to see each other during the times when they are parted.

3:1-5. Still the Shulamite
Her dream: her beloved missing, sought, found

1.   Most commentators take these verses to be the description of a dream. Preoccupied with Solomon all her waking hours, the Shulamite dreams of him! It is a dream where she seeks him everywhere, but cannot find him.

2.   In her dream she gets up, and goes about the city looking for him. But go where she will — through narrow streets, or broader places by the gates, or where the streets cross — he cannot be found. She *must* find him! Her undying love cannot live without him!

3. Moving silently about the unlit streets of ancient cities were the city guards, who stopped and questioned suspicious persons. They approached the Shulamite, but before they could ask her anything, she had blurted out her question to them. Had they seen her beloved?

4-5. But scarcely had she left them when she found him! The dream ends with her embracing him and walking hand in hand with him to her mother's house. She had known what it meant for love to be unsatisfied. Separation had caused it untold pain and measureless grief. It had only found its satisfaction in the presence of the lover. The previously broken heart now welled up with measureless joy. Love is prone to extremes of feeling, and for this reason must be handled with the utmost care. This is why it should not be aroused before the proper time, which is the point of the repeated charge of verse 5.

So runs the first section of Solomon's Song, and as we study it our thoughts are lifted naturally to see two important truths.

The first is that believers find Christ attractive. They rejoice in his love to the unattractive. They are satisfied with him. Nothing pleases them more than to be with him. However poor their view of him may be, there is nothing which they find more thrilling. To them it is the most assuring thought to know that they belong to him. When they are separated from him, their grief is unspeakable. When they find him again, they are overcome with joy.

The second truth is that Christ finds his people attractive. He decks them with beauty, and promises more. He praises his church's loveliness, and nothing less appeals to him. Nothing whatever is more precious to him than his people.

If we cannot see that much in the Song, we must question whether we have any spiritual vision at all. And no doubt there is much more to see, to those with sufficient spiritual enlightenment to lay hold of it.

10.
The wedding   (3:6-5:1)

The Shulamite	Solomon	Onlookers
		3:6-11
	4:1-7	
	4:8-15	
4:16		
	5:1a	
		5:1b

10.
The wedding   (3:6-5:1)

Please read the Song of Solomon 3:6 - 5:1

In the previous section we saw scenes in the courtship days of Solomon and the Shulamite. Now the day of the wedding and its feast has arrived, and we have the privilege of being onlookers as the bridal procession goes past, and of being guests at the celebrations. At no point in our study can we forget that Scripture uses the love relationship which exists between a bridegroom and his bride to describe the relationship which exists between Christ and his people.

In 3:6-11 we observe the bridal pair entering Jerusalem, and afterwards we are at the festivities in the royal palace. 4:1-15 sound a little strange to our Western ears and may even offend our taste. But we need to remember that this kind of song is still sung at Eastern wedding feasts today, especially in Syria, and that no one within that culture is offended by what he hears. This song occupies the longest sub-division in our present section and, as we shall see, divides quite naturally into two parts. It establishes Solomon as the main speaker in this part of the book. We should have expected this. His marriage makes him the head and spokesman of a new household.

There are a number of unique features in this section. For instance, the groom is twice called 'King Solomon' (3:9,11), and six times the Shulamite is called 'spouse' (4:8-12, 5:1) — titles which are not used anywhere else in the book. The word 'come' is of particular importance, and is found at 4:8,16 and 5:1; while there are also four appearances of the word 'garden' (4:12,16, 5:1).

94

3:6-11. *Onlookers*

This sub-division is a description of the bridal procession travelling through the desert to Jerusalem, where 'the day of his espousals' (11), or Solomon's wedding day, is to take place. The event is described as seen through the eyes of the onlookers, who later call upon the whole feminine population of the capital to witness the wedding procession going by (11).

6. 'Who is all this camp?' they excitedly ask, if we translate their question literally. The word 'desert' or 'wilderness' refers to open country, as distinct from cultivated land. As they look across it, perhaps from Jerusalem's walls, they see an immense procession approaching. Its litters and palanquins make it look like a vast moving encampment. In front of it rises a pillar of smoke — no doubt a reference to the incense which was then burned at the head of important processions. On this occasion there were rising the richest and most luxurious perfumes the East could afford. No wonder the crowd was excited! No one had ever seen anything like it before!

7-8. The finer details of the procession became clearer as it came nearer. It was soon possible to point out Solomon's litter, or travelling couch, and to count the number of its escort. In keeping with his royal dignity it consisted of sixty of Israel's finest soldiers. All of them were experienced warriors, capable of protecting the king and his bride from the many dangers to which they might be exposed, especially at night.

9-10. With Solomon's litter now only yards away, the waiting crowd is now able to describe every minute part of it. Its magnificence and royal splendour startle them. It is made of cedar and cypress from Lebanon. The purple or dark red canopy which covers it is held up by silver-covered supports, while the main body of the palanquin is overlaid with gold. The beautiful interior had been both provided and inlaid by the women of Jerusalem themselves as an expression of their love for their king.

11.   What a sight! The call is now given to all the women of Jerusalem to come and behold it, though it is possible that the call is to the waiting bridesmaids to come out and meet the royal procession. Costly crowns were worn at oriental weddings in those days, but who had ever seen one like that which Solomon's mother had placed on his head for this special day? No mention is made of the bride, although she was undoubtedly travelling with Solomon, according to the prevailing custom. She will be the subject of the next chapter, while at the moment all the attention is focused on the groom. His wedding day has arrived! It is to be a day of great joy and gladness, enjoyed by all present to witness it.

4:1-7.   Solomon's first song

What follows is a song praising the unrivalled beauty of the bride. It is dressed in imagery understood and appreciated by the oriental mind, even if not always by others. The whole song is very similar to the *'wasf'* still regularly sung at marriages in Syria. The turbulence of the welcoming crowds is now behind us. The doors have been shut and the wedding has taken place. At this point Solomon rises and publicly praises his bride.

1.   To him she is startlingly beautiful. She has striking eyes which shine through her veil. The black goats, trailing down the hillsides of the fertile pastures just east of Jordan, suggest the dark waves of her beautiful hair.

2.   Her teeth are white, like a flock of newly shorn sheep which have just come up from the washing. Like sets of twins, they correspond perfectly in upper and lower jaws, and none are missing.

3.   'Scarlet' was a bright crimson obtained from an Eastern insect, and 'scarlet thread' vividly describes her thin red lips. Her mouth is really lovely, while her temples are as ruby-coloured as slices of pomegranate.

4.　'The tower of David' was obviously well known at that time, though it can no longer be identified. Presumably Solomon considers her neck to be strong and shapely. It seems probable that the tower was decorated with shields, and that the remainder of the verse compares the many jewels on her neck to these trophies, and remarks how they accentuate her beauty.

5.　In the West a public love poem would not normally include any reference to a woman's breasts. But the Bible does not see anything questionable here, and at this point Eastern culture is still nearer to the Word of God. Like the fawns of the gazelle, the breasts of the bride are youthful and tender. They are a striking feature on an already beautiful scene.

6-7.　The picture now changes to a garden of spices, situated on higher ground, and to a person gathering the precious aromas throughout the day until the blowing of the evening breeze and the fleeing of the daytime's sharp shadows. His aim is to heap all these beautiful fragrances on the one he loves. In the same way Solomon declares that he cannot heap enough praise on his beloved. There is no limit to the beautiful things he could say about her. To him she is nothing less than marvellous. Her beauty and attractiveness are without blemish.

There can be no serious doubting that it is to verse 7 that Paul refers in Ephesians 5:25-27. The church is to Christ what the spouse is to Solomon. He will one day come for his bride and take her to his royal palace. There he will present her to himself, 'a glorious church, not having spot, or wrinkle, or any such thing; but . . . holy and without blemish'.

Our chorus will then be 'Alleluia: for the Lord God omnipotent reigneth. Let us be glad and rejoice, and give honour to him: for the marriage of the Lamb is come, and his wife hath made herself ready' (Revelation 19:6b-7). Our Lord Jesus Christ will spend eternity rejoicing over those he has redeemed.

4:8-15.   Solomon's second song
Solomon's love song is in two parts, and in this second part
he expresses the great longing which he, as the groom, has
for his bride.

8.   Because of his great longing for her, the Shulamite
seems to him to be far away and inaccessible, as if she
were in Lebanon. He calls her to depart from there and to
come to him. Amana is one of the streams that flow east-
wards from the Lebanese mountains, while Mount Hermon,
called Senir by the Amorites, is the highest peak in the
range. To Solomon his bride seems as distant as if she were
in these mountain haunts, and what he wants most in this
world is to have her close beside him.

9.   He finds her beauty irresistible. Just one glance of her
eyes, and but one jewel on her neck, is enough to enrapture
him. The phrase 'my sister' is an expression of unspeakable
preciousness.

10.   He uses language very reminiscent of the language
she used of him in 1:3-4. She gives him immeasurable joy
and gladness — immeasurable pleasure! *This* is what Christ
thinks of his church. He takes pleasure in her graces.

11.   His bride is sweet. She is all that he ever wanted. He
likens her fragrance to that of Lebanon, which was prover-
bial, because of the cedars, shrubs and aromatic herbs
which flourished there.

12.   She belongs exclusively to him, and in that resembles
a walled garden that is locked, and which is therefore inaccessible to all but its owner. To change the metaphor,
but to make the same point, she is described as a well or a
fountain which is sealed, so that only one person can enjoy
its water. He has no other bride, and she has no other husband. She will never belong to anyone else.

13-14.   Here the figure of the garden is continued, and
the same point is underlined. To the king, the Shulamite is

like a garden yielding to its owner the choicest of fruits, which are his, and his alone. Such comparisons are a common feature of *'wasfs'*.

Pomegranates are well known to us, and we have spoken of camphire, spikenard, frankincense and myrrh earlier in the book. Saffron is a form of crocus which is crushed and dried, and used as a condiment. Calamus is an aromatic cane from India and Arabia. Cinnamon originates from Sri Lanka, and is obtained by separating the inner rind from the outer bark of a sort of laurel, and drying it. Aloes are very costly indeed, being obtained from the enormously high eagle wood tree, which gives off a rich perfume when burned.

All of these perfumes and aromatics are exotic. None of them grows naturally in any Palestinian garden. 'The fruits of the Spirit are not native to the sinful heart,' writes W.J. Cameron. What Christ finds attractive in his church is not what grows naturally there, but what divine grace has planted.

15. Just as verses 13 and 14 amplified the first half of verse 12, so this verse amplifies the second part. The king considers his bride to be like fountains and streams which overflow with fresh pure water. She is the source of all his pleasure — a veritable fountain of delight. He draws refreshment from considering her. We are amazed that Paul had *this* chapter in mind when he wrote of the relationship between Christ and his church. He delights in his people in a way which language cannot convey!

4:16.   The Shulamite
This is the only occasion on which the Shulamite speaks in this section, and we have here her response to Solomon's love song. Continuing with the imagery of a garden, she calls both the cool north wind and the warm wind from the south to blow upon her. In this way all the wonderful fragrances which the bridegroom has attributed to her will

stream forth. She is the bridegroom's garden, and she invites her lover to come in and to enjoy the fruits to which he is entitled.

She knows herself to be attractive to him. All his wonderful epithets have fully convinced her of that. She knows she is loved. But she longs to be more attractive still. Close to him, she longs to be even closer. This, too, is every believer's cry. How grateful he is for the promise of John 14:21!

5:1ª. Solomon

Heeding his spouse's call, the king says that he *does* enjoy the excellent fruits of his garden. There *is* union. There *is* communion.

5:1ᵇ. Onlookers

This section closes as it opened, with a cry from the onlookers. 'Eat, friends!' they call to the bride and groom, 'Drink, lovers! Celebrate the joy of your union! Enjoy and delight yourselves in each other's presence!'

Some interpreters take this half of the verse to be an invitation to the wedding. Others think that the couple themselves are speaking, calling on others to join in their joy. Neither of these explanations seems very likely to me. But as a cry from an attending chorus it serves as a fitting climax to the groom's description of his bride, and to her response to it. We leave them as an enraptured couple, revelling in their union as man and wife, and in the loving communion of spirits which binds them so firmly together.

To have allegorized the section we have studied would have been extravagant. Some of us find it impossible to believe that a distinct spiritual meaning is intended, for instance, by every spice and perfume mentioned in 4:13-14. On the other hand, a totally naturalistic interpretation is out of the question, for Paul quite clearly had

this section in mind when he wrote about Christ and his
church in Ephesians 5. We are thus driven back to the
canons of interpretation which we announced in our introduction to the Song. The spiritual mind rises naturally
from a consideration of the poem to a love which is higher
and better.

This section prompts our minds to reflect on what is
revealed elsewhere in the Scriptures, although we stress
again that there is *no exact equivalence* between what we
read there and the poem we are enjoying. Christ's bride
was *chosen* in eternity. Throughout the Old Testament the
wedding was *announced*. When the Son 'of God assumed
our flesh the *betrothal* took place, and at Calvary the
dowry was paid. But what about the *wedding*?

As individuals we enter into union with Christ at the
moment of our conversion. In that sense Christ is already
married to his bride. And yet there are many other men
and women who will be converted in future days. At the
moment they are still in their sins, and others are not yet
even born. God's decree of election has ruled that they will
be joined to Christ, but it has not actually happened yet.
The wedding has yet to take place.

Christ's bride is made up of many individuals, who come
to him one by one. In that sense, the wedding is going on
all the time. When the last of his people has been converted,
the bride will be complete. Then the world will end, and
his bride will be presented to him in the terms described
in Ephesians 5:27. In that sense the wedding is yet to
come. We are repeatedly told of it in our Lord's parables,
but especially in Revelation 19:1-10 and 21:9.

That final marriage supper will be a day of majesty and
glory. It will be marked by the Groom rejoicing over his
bride, by longings satisfied, by unbroken communion, by
perfect expressions of love and by uncontainable joy. Do
we not find that our excitement at such a prospect is stirred
up by this particular part of the Song of songs?

11.
A troubled dream of separation   (5:2-6:3)

The Shulamite	Daughters of Jerusalem
5:2-8	
	5:9
5:10-16	
	6:1
6:2-3	

11.
A troubled dream of separation (5:2-6:3)

Please read the Song of Solomon 5:2 - 6:3

In the section before us the Shulamite recounts a dream that she had not long after her marriage to Solomon. It is a dark section of the book, but it can be a very considerable blessing to our spiritual lives.

In her dream the Shulamite was alienated from Solomon, and went through the most appalling agony of soul until there was a reunion. Apart from two verses spoken by 'the daughters of Jerusalem', the whole of this section is spoken by the Shulamite. Solomon was the principal speaker last time, now it is his bride, and in the closing section of the book they will both speak about equally.

5:2-8. *The Shulamite*

2. The Shulamite's dream took place while she was asleep, but in her dream she was in bed — awake! She dreams that her lover, having made a long journey through the night, and soaked by the heavy Palestinian dew, is outside her door. In the most affectionate terms he asks her to let him in.

3. His words of love meet with a cool response. In her selfishness the Shulamite can only think of what an inconvenient hour it is for such an unexpected arrival. She begins to make the most feeble excuses as to why she should not open the door. She does not even have her underclothes on, and what a bother it will be to put them on again! She has washed her feet clean from the inevitable grime which soiled them during the preceding day. Why should she get

them dirty again? In short, she is tucked up comfortably in bed and resents the thought of having to get out.

4.   Above the lock in the doors of those times was a hole through which the key was inserted. This was frequently large enough to admit the human hand. This verse probably refers to this aperture, or may refer to a small window in the door through which it was possible to speak to those outside. Whichever way it was, Solomon's hand now comes through the hole, as he tries to let himself in. The sight has an immediate effect on the Shulamite. Her reluctance to get up is conquered and she is filled with the strongest longings for Solomon and thrills at the prospect of seeing him.

5.   She now hastens across the room to open the door and fumbles with the lock. The mention of myrrh is probably a figurative way of saying that her hands were filled with welcome. The myrrh referred to is the most highly prized of all, being that which dripped naturally from the tree without any cuts having to be made. It is equally possible that Solomon had perfumed his hands with it, and some of it had dropped onto the latch and handles as he had tried to let himself in, and was now sticking to her hands.

6.   At last the door is swinging open and she expects her eyes to meet those of her beloved. But he has gone! After her initial reluctance the sound of his voice had overwhelmed her, but there is now nobody there! Her disappointment is increased by the knowledge that it is her own cool reception which has discouraged him from remaining. She searches, but there is no sign of him. She calls for him, but there is no reply.

7.   She *must* find him – and goes into the city to continue her search. Eastern women never appear in the streets after nightfall, so it is not surprising that the watchmen were suspicious. They jump out on her, and attack her with the cudgels which they used to arrest forcibly those who did

not respond to their challenges. They tear off her veil to
see who she is. It is a night of shame and humiliation.

8.   At this point the Shulamite makes a charge to the
attending dramatic chorus of 'the daughters of Jerusalem'.
But it is not in the same terms as last time. She has deep
feelings of love, but is unable to find the bridegroom to
convey them. She none the less wants him to know! So if
they find him, will they tell him what she feels? She is
lovesick, pining, fainting and longing. She cannot live
without him.

5:9.   The daughters of Jerusalem

'But what is so special about *him*?' enquires the chorus,
surprised at the message it is asked to convey. 'What is he
like? And in what way is he different from any other man?'

These questions give the Shulamite the opportunity to
describe her beloved's striking and unique appearance.
What follows is virtually another *'wasf'*, and finds many
parallels both in ancient literature and in modern oriental
practice. The Shulamite is going to show that absolutely
everything about her lover is desirable.

5:10-16.   The Shulamite

10.   Like father, like son. David, as a shepherd boy, had
been described as 'ruddy' (1 Samuel 16:12), and the word
is now used of his son. The fair-skinned complexion of
Solomon was fresh and healthily red. This made his appearance so arresting that he was as easily distinguishable as a
standard-bearer surrounded by an army of ten thousand
men.

11.   A nobility radiates from his head and face, which is
accentuated by his curly black hair. Some commentators
think the description is of Solomon wearing a golden-
coloured turban, from which protrude raven-black curls of
hair.

12.   The beauty of the dove is even more pronounced

when it darts into sparkling running water to wash itself. Here the washing is in milk, and the 'doves' are the bridegroom's eyes. The soft, rich, full and moving appearance of his pupils and irises is set off by the whites surrounding them. They look like jewels expertly set in a ring.

13.   A perfumed beard was a sign of strength and honour in the ancient world (see Psalm 133), and Solomon's yielded a unique fragrance. The Shulamite describes his lips as 'lilies' — in this case a very highly-coloured red flower. The words which dropped from them were as precious and valuable as the finest myrrh.

14.   His arms are like rods of gold, tipped with fingernails which resemble jewels such as topaz or chrysolite. And what shall be said of his body? It resembles carved and polished ivory. The description here is not of the naked person, but of the snow-white robe and girdle, set full of jewels, which were a common feature of royal persons in the Orient.

15.   As for his legs, they are like pillars for strength. Marble treated with oil, as it often was, has a fleshly colour, and this explains the reference here. There was even a richness and glory about her lover's footwear. As Lebanon is renowned for its beauty, so his whole aspect is sublime and exalted.

16.   As for his mouth, it is not just finely fashioned, but what flows from it is also wise and noble (see Proverbs 16:21). Every feature of the beloved is altogether lovely. He is without defect, fault or blemish. There is nothing imperfect or spoiled about him. Everything about him is desirable. '*This* is my beloved, and this is my friend,' says the Shulamite of her Solomon, as says the believer of his King. The trusting soul finds Christ entirely attractive, and is able, because of the spiritual discernment granted to him, to recognize his complete perfection.

6:1.   The daughters of Jerusalem

The bride's majestic description of her lover produces an impression on the daughters of Jerusalem, and they immediately desire to join in the search for him. They ask the Shulamite to tell them where he has gone — despite the fact that only a few moments ago she did not know and had asked *them* to relay a message to him, should they find him first.

6:2-3.   The Shulamite

2.   But *this* time she is able to answer! She no longer needs the daughters of Jerusalem to help her in her search. Her bridegroom has gone into his garden. In the light of 4:12-15 and 5:1, where she herself is described as his garden, this can only mean that he has returned to her! If this seems difficult to understand, we should remember that we are reading a dream. This interpretation is confirmed by referring to 4:16, where she describes herself in similar terms to 'the beds of spices' mentioned in this verse. He has come to enjoy what rightly belongs to him.

3.   The relationship is restored. There *is* union. There *is* communion. The absent lover is now being enjoyed by the bride, and is himself enjoying her.

Sometimes Christ withdraws his presence from his people. This is because they lose their first love (Revelation 2:1-7). Something, even if only momentarily, becomes more important to them than their Saviour.

Once he has gone, the believer realizes that he cannot live without him and repents of the unworthy treatment that he has shown him. At such times we search and long for him, and feel that we will die if our fellowship is not renewed soon. Above everything else, we want him to know that we *do* love him.

It is at such moments that we are often brought to face the question: 'What is so special about *him*?' In reply, we begin to describe his excellencies. We talk of his two natures, so mysteriously found in one Person. We reflect on his eternal glory, the depth of his humiliation and the height of his present exaltation. We describe his offices of Prophet, Priest and King. We parade his names and titles, his beauties and graces, and declare that to us who believe, he is precious.

Then suddenly, and to our inexpressible delight, we find that he is with us again! The experience of the Shulamite has become our own! Christ does not absent himself for long from those whose thoughts are filled with him. What happened on the Emmaus Road has been repeated ten thousand times since: 'And it came to pass, that, while they communed together and reasoned, *Jesus himself drew near, and went with them'* (Luke 24:15).

12.
Mutual love   (6:4-8:14)

Solomon	Chorus	The Shulamite
6:4-9		
	6:10	
		6:11-12
	6:13	
7:1-9		
		7:9 - 8:4
8:5 - 14		

12.
Mutual love   (6:4-8:14)

Please read the Song of Solomon 6:4 - 8:14

We have seen the Shulamite reminisce on her courtship days, have attended her wedding and have heard Solomon extol her beauties. Her troubled dream of separation demonstrated to us how close was the bond which bound her and her lover together. The page and a half of the Song which remain show us how the bond grew even stronger as time went by. No relationship of love, including that between the believer and Christ, can remain static. Although the Song actually closes with Solomon and his bride separated from one another, this is no impediment to their revelling and bathing in their mutual love.

The book has thus traced the growth of their love from its beginnings and through its testings to the triumph of its full maturity. To prove that this mature love is truly mutual, no chief speaker is found in this closing section. Bride and groom speak equally, interrupted by several interjections from the ever-attendant chorus.

6:4-9.   Solomon

4.   The section opens with yet another paragraph of praise, in which Solomon praises the Shulamite for her beauty. Tirzah, a city north-west of Samaria, was renowned for its beauty. Perhaps this was the reason why, after Solomon's day, it was chosen as the first capital of the northern kingdom of Israel. Jerusalem, of course, enjoyed an even higher reputation. Solomon found his bride to be as distinctive as that. Like an army with banners, her

unfailing power to attract attention was awesome.

5-7.   One look from her was enough to throw him off balance. It left him overwhelmed, confused and agitated in spirit. Her outstanding beauty is described once more, in terms identical to that of 4:1-3.

8-9.   Just as she herself had seen the king as one who stood out in a company of ten thousand (5:10), so he had to admit that she, too, could simply not be compared with others. However many queens, concubines or maidens might surround her, she always shone out, and they themselves had to acknowledge her beauty as unique and were moved to praise her for it.

It is hard to see any significance in the numbers used in verse 8. Its underlying reference is to the polygamous practices of the time, which were particularly common among the royalty. It furnishes no proof that Solomon himself had descended to polygamy at this stage. His own admission is that the Shulamite is unique. Her beauty is matchless and flawless, and she is the only one for him. The king has only one bride! And our hearts take natural flight to remember that Christ has an undivided love for his church.

6:10.   The Chorus

These words are probably to be understood as the actual words spoken by the women admiring the Shulamite. They see the compelling attractiveness of her appearance to be an increasing, rather than a decreasing quality. The dawn is bright, but brighter still is a moonlit night. Brightest of all is the daytime sun. Are allegorical interpreters wrong to have seen here a reference to the increasing sanctification of the Lord's people?

6:11-12.   The Shulamite

11.   Here the bride responds to the admirers surrounding her by telling them how she came to her present position as the king's bride. She had previously been nothing more

than a peasant girl. In northern Palestine, where she came from, walnuts were common, and one day she went down into the valley to see how the new growth was coming on. She was also looking to see if the vines had budded and whether the pomegranates had blossomed.

12. It was at that point that she became queen! Before she realized it, she had been snatched away to occupy one of the country's royal chariots and to take her place among the royalty. Amazing grace! She is the king's bride, not because of her superior merits, but because of his gracious initiative. She is clearly also telling her admirers that her exceptional beauty is not natural to her, but the result of her having been chosen by the king. Who can miss the spiritual lessons which are to be found here?

6:13.   The Chorus

The admiring women now ask the Shulamite to come back, and to turn and turn again in front of them, so that they can take time to behold her breath-taking features.

We cannot say for certain who asks the question: 'What will ye see in the Shulamite?' Perhaps it is a section of the chorus, or perhaps it is the lover himself. Whichever way it is, the question serves to introduce the next paragraph, where her beauty is described in detail.

There have been scores of attempts to explain the last phrase, which reads in the Authorized Version, 'as it were the company of two armies'. Perhaps it is saying something similar to 6:4b and 10b, where the Shulamite is said to attract attention as much as a flag-carrying army. But it seems more likely that the questioner is asking why they are giving as much attention to her as they would to 'the Mahanaim dance'. This was presumably a well-known and attractive dance, whose movements required a high degree of concentration from the spectators. Some modern versions have opted for this explanation, and it certainly makes good sense. The questioner is asking why everyone is looking at the Shulamite so intently. What do they see in her?

7:1-9ᵃ.   Solomon

1.   We now come to a passage which allegorical scholars have used to show what pleasure the church gives Christ. Solomon is here giving the answer to the question which has just been asked, and does so in a poem extolling the physical beauty of his bride. Although we do not adopt a naturalistic interpretation for this book, we should not forget that the human body is a marvel of God's handiwork and is, accordingly, to be admired. Physical beauty, and physical desire, too, are God-given gifts. Their perversion is undoubtedly degrading, but not the gifts themselves.

The chorus has requested the bride to turn and turn again in front of them, and she is still doing so as Solomon speaks these lines. She may even have been doing the particular dance to which we have just referred. If this is so, some of Solomon's comments become more understandable. He speaks of the beauty of her feet and shoes, and describes her legs, not only as shapely as a carved ornament, but as graceful in movement as a jewelled pendulum. But there is no element of lust or disrespect in what he has to say. To him this beautiful creature is nothing less than a 'prince's daughter' – a term of highest respect and honour at that time.

2.   A goblet was reckoned to be at its most beautiful when it was filled with wine. This is how Solomon sees her 'navel'. It is just possible that this description is to be taken literally, but it is more probable that it is a reference to the whole of the lower part of her body. The colour of wheat was considered to be the most beautiful that a human body could have, though it is virtually certain that it is her dress which is being described here. It was the custom at that time to place heaps of wheat in rows at harvest time, and to decorate them with flowers from the fields. In the same way her dress is decorated with rows of flowers embroidered upon it.

3.   As her breasts were not completely hidden, it was not thought indiscreet to mention them. They are here described in the terms of tender beauty which we have already spoken of in 4:5.

4.   Her neck is as fair and smooth as ivory, and her eyes deep and sparkling, like the large clear pools found by the gate of Bath-rabbim, in the ancient Amorite capital of Heshbon. Not many of us would welcome our nose being described as 'the tower of Lebanon which looketh toward Damascus' — obviously a well known watch-tower of the period! However, we should remember that there have been several periods in history when a prominent nose has been regarded as attractive. As it happens, the word 'nose' may also mean 'face', in which case it is her courageous facial features which are being spoken of.

5.   Her head crowns her excellencies. It is like Mount Carmel, that peak of solitary majesty and grandeur almost on the very shores of the Mediterranean. And who can describe her hair? It is so black that it shines with a purple sheen. Or the idea might be that its colour was striking, for the ancients called any strong and vivid colour by the name of 'purple', because it was their richest colour, and purple dye was an extravagant luxury. The king is held captive and bound by her tresses. The imagery of a lover being held in the locks of the woman he loves is frequently used in Eastern poetry.

6-9a.   Of all things in the world which a person can desire, there is nothing anywhere to compare with his beautiful bride. She is as graceful and as stately as a palm tree, and her breasts are like the clusters of its fruit. He expresses his desire to embrace her, and to enjoy her love and beauty to the full. May he find her breasts welcoming, and may her breath be as fragrant as the highly-valued fragrance of apples. May he discover the touch of her mouth to be as exhilarating to him as wine is to the faint.

7:9b - 8:4.   The Shulamite

9b.   It is worth reading this verse in a modern version. The thought seems to be that while the couple clasp in close embrace, the bridegroom falls asleep. However, the Shulamite remains awake and, continuing with the symbolic language which her lover has just used, she exclaims that her love flows out to him, even while he is asleep. May the wine of her love flow gently over his lips and teeth, and flow straight to his heart of hearts!

10.   She lies there revelling in the fact that she belongs to him, and that she is the one whom he desires. We have here the relaxed and joyful language of assurance. She is confident of his love towards her.

11-12.   As he awakes she urges him that they should escape from everybody and should go into the country, where they can enjoy its sights but, supremely, can also enjoy each other's love without interruption or distraction. Lovers enjoy being alone together. Those who do not enjoy being alone with Christ must sincerely question whether they love him at all.

13.   The mandrake is a plant in the potato family, which produces a sweet-smelling flower in May. Its fruit, somewhat like a plum, was considered to have the power to stimulate sexual desire and to save from barrenness (see Genesis 30:14ff). The mention of this fruit here, together with the promise that she had also stored up every other conceivable fruit for him to enjoy, is all calculated to express her overwhelming desire for him. It is also a clear invitation for him to come and enjoy *her*.

1.   She also desires to have with him the close and intimate relationship which only brothers and sisters know. For instance, if he were her brother, he would be able to kiss her in a public place without calling down public

scorn. It may be of interest to know that still among the
Bedouin today only a brother from the same mother, or a
father's brother's son, have the right to kiss a lady in
public.

2-3.   She longs to bring him home, where they could
drink of the sherbert made from pomegranate juice which
is still popular in some parts of the East today. This
invitation is a picturesque way of expressing a desire for
greater intimacy, which becomes explicit in verse 3, with
its clear announcement of her desire to lie with him in
loving embrace. What believer does not want an increasing
intimacy with his Saviour?

4.   She has chosen that the stirring up of such love is to
be the sole prerogative of the bridegroom, and that no
other person or influence is to have the same effect. There
is here a repetition of the charge given in 2:7 and 3:5.

8:5-14.   Solomon : the Shulamite : the chorus

Up until now the speeches of the various characters in the
book have been distinct and fairly easily identifiable.
There has been a certain separateness about their contri-
butions. As the book now reaches its climax this pattern
breaks down, and the dialogue moves very quickly indeed
from one character to another. There are no more long
speeches, and the final impression created is one of *together-
ness*.

5.   A cry from the *chorus* opens the final scene. The
couple are found walking closely together, in the country.

Solomon reminds the Shulamite how he once found her
sleeping under an apple tree not far from her mother's
house and how he had woken her up. It is quite possible
that he is here recalling their very first meeting.

6-7.   We now hear *the bride* speak, and her words sum up
the entire Song, and provide its climax. She tells the bridegroom that she desires to be his most treasured possession.
'Seals' were signet rings worn on the right hand, bracelets

on the right wrist, or sometimes took the form of a pendant hanging from the neck and over the heart. They indicated authority, or were sometimes mementos of someone especially loved, and were thus regarded as something very precious and dear. This is the place the Shulamite wants to occupy in her lover's affections.

She tells him that her love is so strong that death cannot overcome it. Just as the grave sweeps all before it, so does a lover's jealousy. It will brook no rival. It will not share its lover with another.

Verse 6 is the only place where, in the Hebrew, the name of God appears in this book. Her love burns like 'a flame of God', that is, like an enormous flame. It can never be doused or quenched. But nor can it ever be bought. It is given freely and spontaneously, and anyone trying to purchase it would be scorned. You cannot put a price on love.

8-9.　At this point *the chorus* comes in again, and utters words which, at first sight, seem bizarre and extraordinary. It seems likely that the bride had often recalled words which had been spoken to her some time before by her brothers. These are now taken up and chanted by the chorus. The bride had often remembered the time when her brothers had argued that she was immature and that it was therefore premature to discuss the question of her marrying, although they had admitted that the question would have to be faced one day.

The mention of a 'wall' is probably a picture of the virtue of chastity, and the 'door' is presumably its opposite. The meaning is that if she proved able to keep her suitors at a proper distance, her brothers would strengthen her resolve in every way possible. But if she found it all too easy to yield, they would take the proper measures to defend her in her weakness.

10.　The reply of *the Shulamite* to this is to say that as far as she is concerned, maturity *has* arrived, and the issue of her rejecting or accepting suitors is a living question.

But she will keep them all at bay, except for one. To him
she will surrender, but it will be to him alone. The one
who has a desire towards her shall have all that he desires.
11-12.   She now speaks of this spontaneous self-giving of
herself to Solomon in a totally different way. He had let
out his vineyard at Baal-harmon to a number of tenants.
Whatever fruit they cultivated they could keep for themselves, but they were to compensate Solomon by paying
him 1000 shekels of silver each as an annual rent. The
Shulamite was under no such obligation. She speaks of
herself as a vineyard, which is hers to keep if she wishes.
She does not *have* to give Solomon anything. But she will.
She will give him 1000 shekels — a sum representing the
whole yield of the fruit of her vineyard. It will all be his.
As for those who keep the vineyard on her behalf, she will
pay them two hundred shekels each. In this extravagant
way the Shulamite expresses that Solomon has the first
place in her heart, and that she is voluntarily giving all that
she has, and is, *to him*!
13.   These words move *Solomon,* who now speaks for the
last time. He speaks of his bride as one dwelling in a garden,
surrounded by companions who love to hear her sweet
voice. No less does he! The king's last word to her is that
he wants to hear her voice continually. What a lesson there
is here for the bride of Christ, the church!
14.   The final words of the Song of Solomon are those of
the Shulamite, and are very similar to those found in 2:17.
If you had been writing this love poem, how would you
have ended it? Very probably with an idyllic picture of the
two lovers together in perfect union, bathing in each other's
affection. But the Holy Spirit thought differently. The
closing picture is one of separation. The king has gone
away, and the bride, filled with longing, cannot wait for
him to reappear. People who are truly in love will always
yearn for one another, especially when parted. Separation
serves to increase true love, and not to destroy it.

The last recorded words of the bride express her deepest wish that the king should make haste to return. The parallel between the end of the Song and the close of the book of Revelation is obvious. The heart of the loving believer cries to his absent Lord, 'Come, Lord Jesus.' And we will not be disappointed. Throughout his absence we have in our hands his written promise: 'Surely I come quickly'! (Revelation 22:20).

Other books by

STUART OLYOTT